A Special Study for Children
in
Grades 3 & 4

Learning To Use My Bible

Teacher's Guide

Contains
Reproducible Student Sheets

Joyce Brown

 Abingdon Press

Learning To Use My Bible

A SPECIAL STUDY
FOR CHILDREN IN GRADES 3 & 4

05 06 07 08 – 10 9 8 7 6

MANUFACTURED IN THE UNITED STATES OF AMERICA

Contents

Using This Resource

Many churches present Bibles to children who are beginning third or fourth grade. *Learning to Use My Bible* is designed to help children celebrate this important life passage and to help them make the Bible their lifelong companion.

Learning to Use My Bible does not assume prior knowledge of the Bible on the part of the children or the teacher. The eight-session study is appropriate for children in Grades 3–6.

Basic Resources

The Bible

Each participant will need a copy of the New Revised Standard Version of the Bible.

Teacher Book

Detailed plans for eight sessions, including reproducible activity sheets for students.

Class Pak

Thirty-two pages of games, posters, maps, song charts and more.

Cassette

A 25-minute tape includes songs about the Bible, songs for learning the books of the Bible, and songs based on Bible verses.

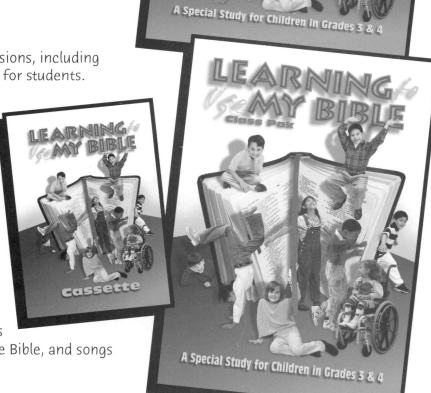

Here's How It Works

•Teacher Book

The lesson plan is divided into three sections:

1. MARK YOUR BIBLE

Offers practice in locating specific Bible books and marking them with a
four-ribbon bookmark that students make in Session 1.

2. USE YOUR BIBLE

Offers instructions for learning centers where students acquire skills that will
help them take responsibility for making the Bible their lifelong companion.
Opportunities for using art, music, games, and research are included each
week.

3. RESPOND TO THE BIBLE MESSAGE

Group activities encourage the students to review learnings and
worship together.

•Reproducible Activity Sheets for Students

Each session includes activity sheets. Using these reproducible sheets, students follow instructions to find and read specific Bible references, then explore the references through creative
activities.

•Cassette

Use of the Cassette is written into the lesson plans as part of the Music Center. Suggestions are
also given for using music when the students worship together.

Class Pak Contents

Try Learning Centers

Learning to Use My Bible is designed so that students may work in learning centers for half the class period.

The learning center approach enables children to acquire skills that will help them take responsibility for making the Bible their lifelong companion. Learning centers:

- Provide self-instruction opportunities.

- Require students to use their Bibles as part of the center activities.

- Let students work at their own pace. Some students will complete work in one center. Others will be able to complete work in four or five centers during the Session.

The learning center approach honors the notion that children learn in many ways. The theory of multiple intelligences (first postulated by Howard Gardner), suggests that everyone is born with the capacity to learn in different ways but that each of us has preferred ways of learning. Gardner has identified seven kinds of intelligence.

- **Verbal/Linguistic** learners enjoy the written and spoken word. Therefore, this curriculum offers reading and writing activities.
- **Logical/Mathematical** learners enjoy reasoning and problem solving. This curriculum offers codes, maps, charts, and games.
- **Visual/Spatial** learners often draw or paint, use maps, or enjoy visualizing. You will find such activities in this curriculum.
- **Musical** learners like to make music and listen to music. This curriculum offers several ways to use the Cassette and Songbook.
- **Kinesthetic** learners enjoy physical activities such as dance, sports, games, signing, building, and crafts. Center activities will address the needs of kinesthetic learners.
- **Interpersonal** learners enjoy talking, leading, and working in groups. As you teach this curriculum, look for ways this type of intelligence is addressed.
- **Intrapersonal** learners enjoy working alone. Some learning centers will suggest working alone, some will suggest working with others.

See Howard Gardner's *Frames of Mind: The Theory of Multiple Intelligences* (Basic Books, 1983) or *7 Ways of Teaching the Bible to Children* by Barbara Bruce (Abingdon Press, 1997).

•Role of Students

- With a learning center approach, students are allowed to move freely through the learning centers, choosing activities that look most interesting to them.
- Once they choose a center, they are to complete the tasks in that center before moving to another center.
- Since each center reinforces the session theme, it is not necessary for a student to visit every center.

•Role of Teacher

- After reading through the session plan, choose which centers you will provide.
- Photocopy and display instructions in the appropriate centers.
- Photocopy the reproducible sheets for students and place them in the appropriate centers.
- Provide any Class Pak resources needed for a specific center.
- Make sure necessary supplies and equipment are available.

Notes on Room Arrangement

• Gathering Place

You will need a gathering space in one part of the room. A circle of chairs near a theme wall works well. If you have a carpeted room, you may want to eliminate the chairs and let students sit on the carpet.

• Learning Centers

You will need several learning centers. Learning centers do not need to be elaborate. A center may be set up at a table, on the floor, on a wall.

• Supplies

Simplify your job by placing basic supplies on open shelves. Encourage students to get the supplies they need (such as pencils, glue, scissors, paint, paper) from the shelves.

Activities for *Learning to Use My Bible* make use of ordinary, readily available supplies. The most costly supplies will be food. Perhaps an adult Sunday school class in your church would like to provide the food suggested each week.

• Equipment

Place a cassette player in the Music Center.

Art: Bob Jones

Song Sheet

The Heavens Tell God's Glory

The heavens tell God's glory, the firmament proclaims the handiwork of God. Creation sings God's name. The moon, the stars, the shining sun, the waters flowing free were spoken into being by majesty's decree.
Oh sing of God's power. Oh tell of God's ways.
Our God is an awesome God,
we bow in humble praise.

Based on selected verses from Psalms 19 and 47. Words by Joyce Brown. © 1998 Abingdon Press.

Teach Me Your Ways, O Lord

Teach me, teach me, teach me your ways, O Lord;
make them known to me; make your ways known to me, O Lord.

Words adapted from Psalm 25:4.

I Treasure Your Word

I treasure your word in my heart, your word is a lamp to my feet.
I treasure your word in my heart, your word is a light to my path.
I delight in your laws, I will not forget your word.
Blessed are you, O Lord. I treasure your word in my heart.

Based on Psalm 119: 11, 12, 16, 105. Words by Joyce Brown. © 1998 Abingdon Press.

The Bible Is a Treasure Book

Bible Passages

Psalm 4:7a -
You have put gladness in my heart.

Psalm 9:1a -
I will give thanks with all my heart.

Psalm 51:10 -
Create a clean heart in me.

Psalm 119:11, 105 -
I treasure your word; your word is a lamp and a light.

Children Will

• gain confidence in locating specific chapters and verses in the Book of Psalms.

• recognize that the Bible offers treasured words for living.

MARK YOUR BIBLE (20 minutes)

• Make Rainbow Bookmarks (Art Center)

Before class enlarge and display the following instructions in the area you have chosen for students to work on art projects:

1. Use the instructions in "Make a Rainbow Ribbon Bookmark" to make a bookmark for your Bible.

2. Complete the activities in "Mark Your Bible."

As the students arrive have them follow the Reproducible 1A instructions for making a rainbow ribbon bookmark and placing the bookmark at the appropriate places in their personal Bibles.

Be available to help individual students. Encourage the students to help each other.

Say: As Christians, we believe that the Bible is our most important book. It is our treasure. In this class we will be learning many things about our treasure book.

Let volunteers define treasure. (Children often think of buried or hidden treasure. If they use that definition, tell them that your class will be digging into the Bible and learning where to look for valuable teachings.)

If some students do not complete this activity at this time, tell them they will have an opportunity to return to the art center later in today's session.

RESOURCES: Bibles; Reproducible 1A; 18-inch strands of red, yellow, green, and blue ribbon; clear tape; paper clips; scissors

• <u>Find the Book of Psalms</u>

Ask the students to bring their Bibles to the gathering circle.

Hold your unopened Bible in your hand and tell the students that you are holding a library in one hand. Explain that the Bible is not just one book, it is a library of 66 books. Tell them that the word Bible comes from the Greek word *Biblia*, which means "books."

Say: We marked the Table of Contents in our Bibles with the red ribbon of our rainbow bookmarks. When we want to find the page where a book of the Bible begins, we can use this Table of Contents. In coming weeks we will learn additional ways to find the books in our Bible.

Using the Table of Contents, show the children that the Bible is divided into two main sections (*Old Testament and New Testament*). Let volunteers name the first book in the Old Testament (*Genesis*), the last book in the Old Testament (*Malachi*), the first book in the New Testament (*Matthew*), and the last book in the New Testament (*Revelation*).

Then, demonstrating with your own Bible, lead the children in following these instructions:

1. Hold your Bible in your lap, spine down and open edge up. Place one hand on each side. With your thumbs, divide the pages in half.

2. Open your Bible. Did you find the Book of Psalms? If not, turn a few pages toward the front or back until you do.
Have the children close their Bibles and find the Psalms several times by trying to open their Bibles in the center.

Tell the children that Psalms, this book in the middle of our Bible, is often called the songbook of our Bible.

Ask: Is the Book of Psalms in the Old Testament or the New Testament? *(Old Testament)*

RESOURCES: Bibles

• <u>Find a Bible Reference</u>

Before class use a black felt-tip marker to write "Psalm 119:105" on newsprint.

Ask the children to find Psalms again and to find the large number(s) on the page where they opened their Bibles. The numbers will vary, depending on which psalm(s) they turned to. Explain that these large numbers are the chapter numbers.

Ask the children to find the smaller numbers, and explain that these are the verse numbers. Explain that every verse of the Bible is numbered.

Show the children the newsprint Bible reference. Explain that a Bible reference tells us where to look to find a specific part of the Bible.

Using the red marker, underline *Psalm*. Tell the children this is the name of the book of the Bible. Using the green marker, underline *119*; and tell them the number after the word *Psalm* tells which large number to look for. Have everyone find Psalm 119 in his or her Bible.

Using the blue marker, underline *105*. Explain that the number after the colon (:) tells which verse (105) to find. Have everyone find the verse and let a volunteer read the verse aloud.

Let volunteers tell what they think this verse means. Help them understand that the Bible is often called God's Word and that the Bible gives us guidance for life.

Have the children move the green ribbon of their rainbow bookmarks to the page where they found Psalm 119:105. Then lead the group in a unison reading of this verse.

RESOURCES: Bibles; newsprint; black, red, green, and blue felt-tip markers

• Prepare to Work in Centers

Show the children that you have provided several learning stations where they may work.

Tell them they may choose the center where they wish to work first. Tell them they should complete the activities in one center before moving to another center.

Show them where supplies are stored. Tell them they may get the supplies they need. Ask them to return supplies to the shelves when they have finished an activity.

Remind them that class members worked in the Art Center as they arrived. If some students did not complete the bookmark or use the ribbons to mark specific Bible books, encourage them to return to the Art Center and complete that work before choosing another center.

USE YOUR BIBLE (30 minutes)

Permission is granted to enlarge and display the instructions for the four learning center stations described in this section.

• Sing and Sign a Bible Verse (Music Center)

1. Read Psalm 119:105 in your Bible.

2. Using the Cassette recording and the words on the Class Pak Chart, sing "Thy Word Is a Lamp." First listen to the song; then play it again and sing along.

3. Sing the song again and try to sign it while you sing. Stand face-to-face with a friend and practice signing the words until you can sign them from memory.

RESOURCES: Bibles, Cassette, cassette player, Class Pak—pp. 14 & 19

• <u>Enjoy Heart Snacks</u> (Food Center)

1. Read Psalm 51:10 in your Bible.

2. Read Psalm 119:11 in your Bible.

3. Place a candy ball on wax paper. Shape the ball into a heart.

4. Eat your candy heart as you read Psalm 119:11 again from your Bible.

RESOURCES: Bibles; 6-inch squares of wax paper; cream cheese candy balls made from this recipe: Combine 2 cups powdered sugar, 2 ounces cream cheese, and 1/4 teaspoon vanilla flavoring. Form into 2-inch balls.

• <u>Crack the Code</u> (Research Center)

1. Follow instructions in "Find Hidden Treasures."

2. Which decoded Bible verse do you like best?

3. Write that verse on a slip of paper. Be sure to include the Bible reference (Psalm ___:___a).

4. Fold the Bible-verse paper several times and bury it in the tray of sand.

RESOURCES: Bibles, Reproducible 1B, paper, pencils, a tray of sand (a plastic dish pan or a plastic shoe box will work well)

• <u>Play Bible Brain</u> (Game Center)

Play the game with others in this center. Directions are printed on the gameboard (Class Pak—pp. 16–17).

Before class: Cut out the game cards, then assemble the counting cube and game markers, from Class Pak—p. 11. Display the Old Testament Library and the New Testament Library (Class Pak—pp. 3 & 5).

RESOURCES: Class Pak—pp. 3 & 5, 11, 16–17

RESPOND TO THE BIBLE MESSAGE
(10 minutes)

Ask the students to bring their Bibles and any reproducible sheets they completed to the gathering circle.

• Review Learning Center Work

Use the following ideas to review some work done in learning centers:

1. Game Center: Read the questions from several cards from "Bible Brain Game," letting volunteers answer. Express appreciation for how much class members have learned today about our treasure book, the Holy Bible.

2. Research Center: Let volunteers share their answers from "Find Hidden Treasures" (Reproducible 1B). Remind the students that our Bible is filled with treasured words. Explain that in today's session, they have read treasured words from the Book of Psalms.

3. Music Center: Let volunteers sing and sign "Thy Word Is a Lamp."

RESOURCES: Bibles, game cards from Bible Brain Game, Reproducible 1B, Class Pak—pp. 14 & 19, Cassette, cassette player

• Worship Together

Show the sign: "Our Bible, a Treasure Book" (Class Pak—p. 2). Let a volunteer tape the sign to the wall in your gathering area.

Say: We will leave this sign on our wall to remind us that this library we can hold in our hand is filled with treasured words.

Ask the students to listen as you play the Cassette recording of "I Treasure Your Word." Ask if anyone has heard the words of this song before. (The song is based on selected verses from Psalm 119. The students read Psalm 119:11 in the Food Center and in the Research Center today. They read Psalm 119:105 in the Music Center.)

Distribute Song Sheets (copied from page 9 in this book). Have them find the words to "I Treasure Your Word." Using the Cassette for accompaniment, lead the students in singing "I Treasure Your Word." Save the Song Sheets for use in later sessions.

Let a volunteer dig up a Bible verse slip buried in the tray of sand. Have the volunteer read the verse aloud three times (including the Bible reference), then see if the class can repeat that verse from memory (with Bible reference).

Close with prayer, giving thanks for God's Word, for minds able to learn new things, and for hearts willing to treasure God's word.

RESOURCES: Class Pak—p. 2, tray of sand with buried Bible verses (from the Research Center), Cassette, cassette player, Song Sheets photocopied from page 9 in this book

Make a Rainbow Ribbon Bookmark

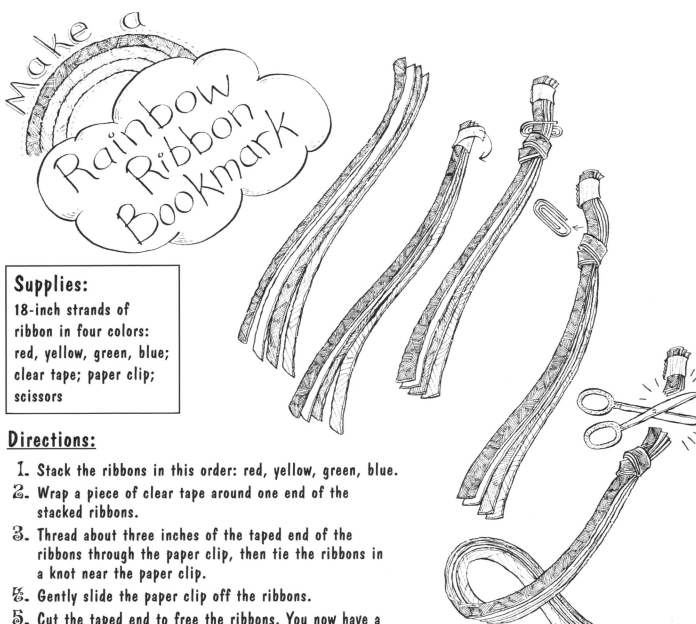

Supplies:
18-inch strands of ribbon in four colors: red, yellow, green, blue; clear tape; paper clip; scissors

Directions:

1. Stack the ribbons in this order: red, yellow, green, blue.
2. Wrap a piece of clear tape around one end of the stacked ribbons.
3. Thread about three inches of the taped end of the ribbons through the paper clip, then tie the ribbons in a knot near the paper clip.
4. Gently slide the paper clip off the ribbons.
5. Cut the taped end to free the ribbons. You now have a rainbow bookmark.

Mark Your Bible

1. Find and mark the Table of Contents in your Bible, using the red ribbon.
2. Use the yellow ribbon to mark Genesis, the first book in the Old Testament.
3. Use the green ribbon to mark the Book of Psalms, the middle of the Bible.
4. Use the blue ribbon to mark Matthew, the first book in the New Testament.

1-A

FIND HIDDEN TREASURES

Each Bible book contains many verses. Some verses stand out in our memory more than others. They are like hidden treasures that we find. Sometimes only a part of a verse stands out in our memory.

When we see a lowercase letter "a" after the number of the Bible verse, we read only the first part of the Bible verse.

Use the heart code to complete the Bible verses on this page. To check your work, find and read each verse in your Bible.

You have put G L A D N E S S in my heart. (Psalm 4:7a)

I will give T H A N K S to the LORD with my whole heart. (Psalm 9:1a)

Create in me a C L E A R heart, O God. (Psalm 51:10a)

I T R E A S U R E your word in my heart. (Psalm 119:11a)

Art: Bob Jones

2 A Special Library

Bible Passages

Psalm 119:105 - Your word is a lamp and a light.

Psalm 143:10 - Teach me to do your will.

Jonah 2:1 - Jonah prayed.

Matthew 9:9 - Jesus called Matthew.

John 3:16 - God so loved the world that he sent Jesus.

Children Will
- learn that the Bible is a library with different kinds of literature.
- recognize that we believe the Bible is a holy book, inspired by God.

MARK YOUR BIBLE (10 minutes)

• Use Rainbow Ribbon Bookmarks

Before class write the following on the chalkboard:
Jonah 2 - yellow ribbon
Psalm 143 - green ribbon
Matthew 9 - blue ribbon

As the students arrive tell them to use the ribbons of their rainbow bookmarks (made last week) to mark the Bible references. Encourage them to use their Table of Contents to find the page where each Bible book begins.

Remind them that the number immediately following the Bible book name is a chapter number and will be printed in larger type in their Bibles.

Students who were absent last week will need to make a four-ribbon Bible bookmark. Ask the students who made bookmarks last week to show others how to make the bookmarks and how to use the red ribbon to mark the Table of Contents. If they need help, have them refer to Reproducible 1A from last week.

As students finish marking their Bible references, tell them they have 30 minutes to work in the learning centers you have set up in the classroom. Remind them to get the supplies they need for a center and to return the supplies when they have finished. Remind them to complete the activities in one center before moving to another center.

RESOURCES: Bibles; rainbow ribbon bookmarks made last week; a copy of Reproducible 1A; 18-inch strands of red, yellow, green, and blue ribbon; clear tape; paper clips; scissors; chalkboard and chalk

Permission is granted to enlarge and display the instructions for the six learning center stations described in this section.

• <u>Shelve the Library Books</u> (Art Center)

1. Read Psalm 143:10.

2. Follow instructions in "Bible Library."

3. Follow instructions in "Return the Books."

> RESOURCES: Bibles; Reproducible 2A and 2B; pencils; crayons or colored pencils in six colors: red, yellow, green, orange, blue, and purple

• <u>Sing and Sign a Bible Verse</u> (Music Center)

1. Read Psalm 119:105 in your Bible.

2. Using the Cassette recording and Class Pak Chart, sing "Thy Word Is a Lamp."

3. Use the sign language when you sing. If you did not learn the song last week, practice with a friend until you can sign it from memory.

> RESOURCES: Bibles, Cassette, cassette player, Class Pak—pp. 14 & 19

• <u>Enjoy Stories and a Snack</u> (Food Center)

1. Our Bible is filled with stories. Read Jonah 2:1.

2. While you eat three fish crackers, tell a friend everything you can remember about the story of Jonah, who was swallowed by a great big fish.

3. Read Matthew 9:9. Tell a friend how many disciples Jesus called to follow him. Eat that many fish crackers.

> RESOURCES: Bibles, a bowl of goldfish crackers, napkins

• <u>Crack the Code</u> (Research Center)

1. Read John 3:16 in your Bible.

2. Follow instructions in "Most Popular Book."

3. Follow instructions in "The Scriptures Speak in Many Languages."

RESOURCES: Bibles, pencils, Reproducible 2C & 2D

• <u>Play Bible Books</u> (Game Center 1)

Use these rules for Bible Books Game 1 (Old Testament/New Testament) to play this game with friends.

RESOURCES: game cards from Class Pak— pp. 7 & 26, game directions from page 87 in this book

• <u>Play Bible Brain</u> (Game Center 2)

Play the game with others in this center. Directions are printed on the gameboard (Class Pak—pp. 16-17).

Before class: If you did not offer this game last week, cut out the cards and assemble the counting cube and game markers from Class Pak—p. 11. Display the Old Testament Library and the New Testament Library (Class Pak—pp. 3 & 5)

RESOURCES: Class Pak—pp. 3 & 5, 11, 16 & 17

RESPOND TO THE BIBLE MESSAGE
(20 minutes)

Ask the students to bring their Bibles and any reproducible sheets they completed to the gathering circle.

• <u>Find Some Bible Books</u>

Say: **While you worked in centers today, you used your Bible's Table of Contents to find things in four** different Bible books: Psalms, Jonah, Matthew, and John. Who remembers how we found the Book of Psalms last week without using the Table of Contents?

Let a volunteer demonstrate finding Psalms by opening the Bible in the middle.

Tell the children we can use this method to find other books also. Then, demonstrating with your own Bible, lead the children in following instructions 1-6 on Class Pak—p. 28 to find Psalms, Deuteronomy, and Matthew. Be sure to include this poster's information about the type books they will hold in left hands and right hands.

RESOURCES: Bibles, Class Pak—p. 28

• Review Learning Center Work

Say: God wants us to use our Bibles and our brains. Let's see how much we have learned today.

Use the following ideas to review some work done in learning centers:

1. Art Center: Let volunteers answer as you read aloud Reproducible 2A. Then let volunteers name a book of law, a book of history, a book of poetry, a prophet book, a gospel book, a letter. (Use Reproducible 2B to check their answers.)

2. Music Center: Let volunteers show the sign language for Psalm 119:105.

3. Food Center: Let a volunteer tell how many disciples Jesus called to follow him. (*twelve*)

4. Research Center: Let volunteers answer as you read aloud Reproducible 2C.

5. Bible Books Game: Hold up a few cards and let the children name each book as an Old Testament or New Testament book.

6. Bible Brain Game: Ask a few questions from game cards.

RESOURCES: Reproducible 2A, 2B, 2C; game cards from Bible Books Game and from Bible Brain Game

• Worship Together

Show the children your Bible.

Say: The stories and teachings of the Bible were told for many years before they were written down. Parents told them to their children, who told them to their children. We believe that God helped the people remember the stories and teachings. Later, people began to write the stories and teachings down; they knew that people needed help in remembering what God wanted them to do. We believe that God inspired people to write the Bible teachings. We also believe that God inspires us to read and to understand the Bible today.

Let volunteers define *inspired* (*when God's spirit helps us know the right thing to do*).

Ask the children to look at the outside cover of their Bibles and tell what they see. Most should find the words "Holy Bible." Let volunteers define *holy* (*something that belongs to God, something that comes from God*).

Conclude: The Bible is our holy book. Our Bible comes from God, who inspired people to write down God's teachings, and who inspires us to read and understand God's teachings.

Have the students stand in a circle. Hold up your Bible.

Remind the students that the stories and teachings of the Bible are passed from one generation of people to the next. Tell them that the song "Wonderful Book of God's People" calls the Bible a book full of pages "passed down through the ages."

Say: As we listen to the song, let's see if we can pass my Bible around the circle. Let's try to pass it in rhythm to the song. Let's try not to drop our holy book. Let's listen carefully to the words of the song as we pass the Bible.

Join the children in listening to the song and passing the Bible around the circle. Then challenge them to listen to the song again as they pass two copies of the Bible around the circle without dropping them. If the children enjoy this activity, repeat a third time, using three Bibles and encouraging the students to sing along with the recording.

Close with prayer giving thanks that members of your class are on a life-long journey of using the Bible. Ask God to help you spend the rest of your lives learning from the Bible, our holy book.

RESOURCES: Bibles, Cassette, cassette player

Bible Library

The Bible is a library you can hold in your hand. Each Bible book has its own name and place in the Bible library.

Different books in the Bible library have different kinds of writings. Some give God's laws. Some tell stories of history. Some are songs or poems. Some have warnings. Some tell about Jesus. Some are letters.

Some books are in the Old Testament. Some books are in the New Testament. Use the Table of Contents in your Bible to count:

_____ books are in the Old Testament

_____ books are in the New Testament

_____ books are in the Bible

Return the Books

Some books are missing. Use the Table of Contents in your Bible to name the missing books. Write the correct names in the empty book spaces.

Color the books on the shelf as follows:

Law — red
History — yellow
Poetry and **Songs** — green
Prophets — orange
Gospels — blue
Letters — purple

Genesis, Leviticus, Numbers, Deuteronomy

LAW

Joshua, Judges, 1 Samuel, 2 Samuel, 1 Kings, 1 Chronicles, 2 Chronicles, Nehemiah, Esther

HISTORY

Job, Proverbs, Ecclesiastes, Song of Solomon

POETRY AND SONG

Isaiah, Jeremiah, Lamentations, Ezekiel, Daniel, Hosea, Joel, Obadiah, Jonah, Nahum, Habakkuk, Zephaniah, Haggai, Zechariah, Malachi

PROPHETS

Matthew, Luke, John

GOSPELS

Acts

HISTORY

1 Corinthians, 2 Corinthians, Philippians, Colossians, 1 Thessalonians, 2 Thessalonians, 1 Timothy, 2 Timothy, Philemon, Hebrews, James, 1 Peter, 2 Peter, 1 John, 2 John, 3 John, Revelation

LETTERS

Most Popular Book

The Bible is the most popular book in the world. There are more than TEN BILLION COPIES OF THE BIBLE in the world today. If placed end to end, they would go all the way to the moon and back twice! Use the sign language code to discover more about the world's most popular book.

The Old Testament was first written in the
H E B R E W language.

The New Testament was first written in the
G R E E K language.

Over the years the Bible has been translated into
almost T W O

T H O U S A N D languages.

The Scriptures Speak in Many Languages

Read John 3:16 from your Bible.

People in many lands read the Bible in their own languages. Can you read the languages below?

English

For God so loved the world that he gave his only Son, so that everyone who believes in him may not perish but may have eternal life.

John 3:16

Korean

하나님이 세상을 이처럼
사랑하사 독생자를 주셨으니
이는 그를 믿는 자마다
멸망하지 않고 영생을
얻게 하려 하심이라

Spanish

Porque de tal manera amó Dios al mundo, que ha dado a su Hijo unigénito, para que todo aquel que en él cree, no se pierda, mas tenga vida eterna.

Juan 3:16

New Testament
Greek

Οὕτως γὰρ ἠγάπησεν ὁ θεὸς
τὸν κόσμον, ὥστε τὸν υἱὸν τὸν
μονογενῆ ἔδωκεν, ἵνα πᾶς ὁ
πιστεύων εἰς αὐτὸν μὴ ἀπόληται
ἀλλ᾽ ἔχῃ ζωὴν αἰώνιον.

3 *The Old Testament: God's Mighty Acts*

Bible Passages

Genesis 1:1-13 -
God created the heavens and the earth.

Exodus 20:1-17 -
God gives the Ten Commandments.

Psalm 8:3-4 -
When I look at the heavens, what are human beings?

Psalm 19:1 -
The heavens tell of God's glory.

Psalm 47:2 -
God is awesome.

Children Will

- read a portion of the creation story from Genesis 1.
- learn to find the Ten Commandments
- discover psalms giving praise for God's mighty acts

MARK YOUR BIBLE (10 minutes)

• Use Rainbow Ribbon Bookmarks

Before class write Genesis 1:1-5 on newsprint and the following on the chalkboard:
Genesis 1 - yellow ribbon
Exodus 20 - green ribbon
Psalm 19 - blue ribbon

As the students arrive tell them to use the ribbons of their rainbow bookmarks (made in Session 1) to mark the Bible references. Encourage them to use the Table of Contents to find the page where each Bible book begins.

Remind them that the number immediately following the Bible book name is a chapter number and will be printed in large type in their Bibles.

If some students have not yet made a four-ribbon Bible bookmark, let volunteers show them how to make the bookmarks and how to use the red ribbon to mark the Table of Contents. If they need help, refer them to a copy of Reproducible 1A.

As students finish marking their Bibles, show them the newsprint where you have written Genesis 1:1-5. Tell them to read Genesis 1:1-5 silently. If students need help, tell them that the hyphen (-) tells them to begin with verse 1 and to read all the way to the end of verse 5.

Tell the students that they will have 30 minutes to work in the learning centers. Remind them to complete the activities in one center before moving to another center.

RESOURCES: Bibles, rainbow ribbon bookmarks (made in Session 1), a copy of Reproducible 1A, newsprint and a felt-tip marker or chalkboard and chalk.

Permission is granted to enlarge and display the instructions for the six learning center stations described in this section.

• <u>Create A Picture</u> (Art Center)

Follow instructions in "God's Mighty Acts: Creation."

RESOURCES: Bibles, copies of Reproducible 3A, watercolor paints, brushes, water

• <u>Sing About Old Testament Books</u> (Music Center)

1. Find the Table of Contents in your Bible.

2. As you listen to the Cassette recording of "Old Testament Books," read the names of the books from the Table of Contents in your Bible.

3. Then sing along with the Cassette recording.

RESOURCES: Bibles, Cassette, cassette player

• <u>Enjoy Manna</u> (Food Center)

1. Follow instructions in "Manna and More."

2. Then slice a small piece from the manna loaf and eat it.

RESOURCES: Bibles; Reproducible 3B; pencils; a knife; napkins; a manna loaf made from this recipe: Blend together 1/4 cup honey, 1/4 cup peanut butter, 1/2 cup dry milk solids, 3/4 cup graham cracker crumbs. Shape into a log, wrap in wax paper, and chill. Yields 12 small slices.

• Crack the Code (Research Center)

1. Follow instructions in "Our Awesome God."

2. Which decoded Bible verse do you like best?

3. Write that verse on a slip of paper. Be sure to include the Bible reference (Psalm __:__).

4. Fold the Bible-verse paper several times, and bury it in the tray of sand.

RESOURCES: Bibles, pencils, Reproducible 3C, paper, tray of sand (used in Session 1)

• Play Bible Books (Game Center 1)

To play this game today, use the rules for Bible Books Game 2 (Literature Type).

RESOURCES: Old Testament game cards (1-39) from Class Pak—pp. 7 & 26, copy of game directions from page 87 in this book

• Play Bible Toss (Game Center 2)

Play the game with others in this center. Be sure to keep your own score.

Before class: Display the Old Testament Library Poster (Class Pak—p. 3). Assemble the Bible Toss gameboard from Class Pak—p. 9, using the "Get Ready" instructions from page 88 in this book. Punch out the playing cards from Class Pak—p. 22. Provide game markers (coins or buttons), slips of paper and pencils, and the game instructions.

RESOURCES: Class Pak—pp. 3, 9, 22; copy of game directions from page 88 in this book

RESPOND TO THE BIBLE MESSAGE
(20 minutes)

Ask the students to bring their Bibles and any reproducible sheets they completed to the gathering circle.

• Find Some Bible Books

Say: Today we found Bible passages in the Old Testament part of our Bible. We read verses from the first book in our Bible (Genesis), the second book in our Bible (Exodus), and from the nineteenth book in our Bible (Psalms). Who remembers how we find the Book of Psalms without using the Table of Contents?

Let a volunteer demonstrate finding Psalms by opening the Bible in the middle.

Remind the children we can use this method to find other books also. Then, demonstrating with your own Bible, lead the children in following instructions 1-6 on Class Pak—p. 28 to find Psalms, Deuteronomy, and Matthew.

RESOURCES: Bibles, Class Pak—p. 28

• Review Learning Center Work

Say: The Old Testament portion of our Bible contains many stories about God's mighty acts. Today we read about God's mighty act of creating the world. We read about God's mighty act of saving the people from slavery in Egypt and of providing food for them while they wandered 40 years in the wilderness. We read about God's mighty act of giving special laws to the people. We read psalms praising God's mighty acts.

Use the following ideas to review some work done in learning centers:
1. Art Center: Let volunteers answer as you read aloud Reproducible 3A. Let volunteers show their pictures.

2. Music Center: Let a volunteer name the five books of law. Let others name one of the twelve books of history, one of the five books of poetry, or one of the seventeen prophet books. (Use the Old Testament Library Poster [Class Pak—p. 3] to check their answers.)

3. Food Center: Let volunteers answer as you read aloud Reproducible 3B.

4. Research Center: Let volunteers answer as you read aloud Reproducible 3C.

RESOURCES: Reproducible 3A, 3B, and 3C; Class Pak—p. 3; some game cards from Bible Books Game and from Bible Toss Game

5. Bible Books Game: Hold up a few Old Testament cards and let the children tell what type literature the book is.

6. Bible Toss Game: Ask a few questions from the game cards.

• <u>Worship Together</u>

Let a volunteer dig up a Bible verse slip buried in the tray of sand. Have the volunteer read the verse aloud three times (including the Bible reference), then see if the class can repeat that verse from memory (with Bible reference).

NOTE: The number of buried Bible verses in this tray is growing because students buried verses during Session 1 also. If time allows, you may want to let a second volunteer dig up a verse and lead the class is this cooperative Bible memorizing activity.

Ask the students to listen as you play the Cassette recording of "The Heavens Tell God's Glory." Ask if anyone has heard the words of this song before. (The song is based on selected verses from Psalm 19 and Psalm 47, which the students read today in the Research Center.)

Ask the students to close their eyes and paint imaginary pictures on the inside of their eyelids as they listen to the song a second time. Play the recording again.

Then ask the students to join you in a directed prayer.

Say: We will pray silently to our awesome God. Let us offer silent prayers, thanking God for some part of creation. (pause) Let us thank God for creating each of us as a special child of God. (pause) Let us thank God for guiding our lives. (pause) Amen.

RESOURCES: Tray of sand with buried Bible verses (from the Research Center), Cassette, cassette player

God's Mighty Acts:
Creation

The first story in our Bible tells about one of God's mighty acts—creating the world.
Use Genesis 1:1 in your Bible to answer:

In the beginning . . . God created the _____

and the _____.

In the space below paint a picture of something God made on day 3 of creation
(read Genesis 1:9-13 if you need help).

3-A

MANNA and MORE

The second book in our Bible, Exodus, tells of God's mighty acts. Do you remember the story of God and Moses?

God heard the groaning of the Israelites who were living as slaves in Egypt. God spoke from a burning bush and told Moses to go to Egypt and rescue the slaves. God told Moses to lead the Israelites out of Egypt. God told Moses to lead the Israelites to the land of Canaan. God promised to give the Israelites a new land, the land of Canaan.

The journey to Canaan took forty years. As the Israelites traveled, God provided for them. God gave them food. Each night quail flew into their camp, so that the people had meat. Each morning the ground was covered with a white substance that the people gathered and made into bread. The people called manna, tasted like it was made with honey.

God also provided laws to help the people live the way God wanted them to live. We call these laws the Ten Commandments. Read Exodus 20:1-17 to fill in the missing words of the Ten Commandments.

You shall have no other _____ before me. (verse 3)

You shall not make for yourself an _____. (verse 4)

You shall not make wrongful use of the _____ of the LORD. (verse 7)

Remember the _____ day, and keep it holy. (verse 8)

Honor your _____ and your _____. (verse 12)

You shall not _____. (verse 13)

You shall not _____ adultery. (verse 14)

You shall not _____. (verse 15)

You shall not bear _____ witness against your neighbor. (verse 16)

You shall not _____. (verse 17)

3-B

Our Awesome God

The Bible tells many stories about God's mighty acts.

God created the heavens and the earth.

God delivered the Israelite people from slavery in Egypt and led them to the promised land of Canaan. Bible people often lived outdoors and sometimes slept under the sky.

Use the star code to discover some words about our awesome God.

Use the Bible references to check your work.

| a | d | e | f | g | h | i | k | m | n | o | r | s | t | v | w | y |

When I look at your H E A V E N S, the work of your F I N G E R S,

the moon and the stars that you have established; what are human beings that you are mindful of them, mortals that you care for them? (Psalm 8:3-4)

The H E A V E N S are telling the glory of God; and the firmament

proclaims his H A N D I W O R K. (Psalm 19: 1)

For the LORD, the Most High, is A W E S O M E,

a great king over all the E A R T H. (Psalm 47:2)

3-C

The Old Testament: Judges, Kings, Prophets

Bible Passages

Judges 4:4-5 - Deborah judges the Israelites.

1 Samuel 7:5-6 - Samuel judges the Israelites.

1 Kings 2:11 - David reigns forty years.

1 Kings 4:32 - Solomon writes proverbs and songs.

Psalm 25:4 - Make me to know your ways.

Proverbs 17:17a, 22:6 - A friend loves. Train children.

Amos 5:24a - Let justice roll like water.

Micah 6:8 - What does God require?

Children Will

• learn that some Old Testament history books tell the story of judges and kings.

• learn that Old Testament prophet books tell about persons who were called to speak God's message.

• acknowledge their need to learn from God.

MARK YOUR BIBLE (10 minutes)

• Use Rainbow Ribbon Bookmarks

Before class write the following on the chalkboard:
Judges 4 - yellow ribbon
1 Kings 2 - green ribbon
Amos 5 - blue ribbon

As the students arrive tell them to use the ribbons of their rainbow bookmarks (made in Session 1) to mark the Bible references. Encourage them to use the Table of Contents to find the page where each Bible book begins.

Show them that two Old Testament books have the name "kings." Tell them that we say "First Kings" and "Second Kings" instead of saying "One Kings" and "Two Kings."

Remind them that the number immediately following the Bible book name is a chapter number and will be printed in large type in their Bibles.

Tell them that they will have 30 minutes to work in the learning centers. Remind them to complete the activities in one center before moving to another center.

RESOURCES: Bibles, rainbow ribbon bookmarks (made in session 1), chalkboard and chalk

Permission is granted to enlarge and display the instructions for the seven learning center stations described in this section.

• Reveal a Message (Art Center)

Follow instructions in "Amos: The Prophet of Justice."

RESOURCES: Bibles, copies of Reproducible 4A, white crayons, watercolor paints, brushes, water

• Sing About Old Testament Books (Music Center)

1. Find the Table of Contents in your Bible.

2. As you listen to the Cassette recording of "Old Testament Books," read the names of the books from the Table of Contents in your Bible.

3. Then sing along with the Cassette recording.

RESOURCES: Bibles, Cassette, cassette player

• Take Twelve (Food Center)

1. The people of Israel were divided into twelve tribes. There are twelve history books in the Old Testament.

2. Eat twelve grapes as you follow instructions in "Life in Canaan."

3. On the map find the place where Deborah judged, the place where Samuel prayed, and the places where David lived while he was king.

RESOURCES: Bibles, Reproducible 4B, pencils, Class Pak—p. 27, grapes (12 per student)

- ## Crack the Code (Research Center 1)

Follow instructions in "Micah's Message."

RESOURCES: Bibles, pencils, Reproducible 4C

- ## Gain Wisdom (Research Center 2)

Follow instructions in "Wise Words."

RESOURCES: Bibles, pencils, crayons, Reproducible 4D

- ## Play Bible Books (Game Center 1)

To play this game today, use the rules for Bible Books Game 2 (Literature Type).

RESOURCES: Old Testament game cards (1-39) from Class Pak— pp. 7 & 26, copy of game directions from page 87 in this book

- ## Play Bible Toss (Game Center 2)

Play the game with others in this center. Be sure to keep your own score.

RESOURCES: If you did not offer this game last week, see page 30 for resources you will need.

RESPOND TO THE BIBLE MESSAGE
(20 minutes)

Ask the students to bring their Bibles and any reproducible sheets they completed to the gathering circle.

• Find Some Bible Books

Let a volunteer demonstrate finding Psalms by opening the Bible in the middle.

Remind the children that we can use this method to find other books also. Demonstrating with your own Bible, lead the children in following instructions 1-6 on Class Pak—p. 28 to find Psalms, Deuteronomy, and Matthew. Be sure to include this poster's information about the type books they are holding in left hands and right hands.

RESOURCES: Bibles, Class Pak—p. 28

• Review Learning Center Work

Say: Again today we read verses from the Old Testament section of our Bible. Last week we read about God giving special laws to the Israelite people. What do we call those laws? (*the Ten Commandments*)

Continue: Bible people needed to remember those laws. They needed to obey those laws. But they often broke those laws. God chose leaders to help the Israelites. First God chose judges, later God chose kings. The twelve history books of the Old Testament are filled with stories about those judges and kings. God also chose prophets. We have seventeen prophet books in the Old Testament.

Use the following ideas to review some work done in learning centers:
1. Art Center: Allow volunteers to show their pictures and read the message of Amos 5:24a.

2. Music Center: Let volunteers name some of the twelve history books and some of the seventeen prophet books. (Use the Old Testament Library Poster to check their answers.)

3. Food Center: Let volunteers answer as you read aloud Reproducible 4B. Let others find each place on the Class Pak Map as the answer is read. Ask the students why they think they were told to eat twelve grapes? (twelve books of history, twelve tribes of Israel)

4. Crack the Code: Let a volunteer read Micah's Message (Reproducible 4C).

5. Gain Wisdom: Let volunteers answer as you read aloud Reproducible 4D.

RESOURCES: Reproducible 4A, 4B, 4C, 4D; Class Pak—pp. 3, 27; some game cards from Bible Books Game and from Bible Toss Game

6. Bible Books Game: Hold up a few Old Testament cards and let the children tell what type literature the book is.

7. Bible Toss Game: Ask a few questions from the game cards.

• <u>Worship Together</u>

Ask the students to listen as you play the Cassette recording of "Teach Me Your Ways, O Lord." Ask what Bible persons might have prayed these words to God. (*King Solomon; also any of the judges, kings, or prophets, as well as Bible people whose names we do not know*)

Have the students find Psalm 25 in their Bibles. Ask who wrote this psalm (*authorship is assigned to David, who became the second king of Israel*). Let a volunteer read Psalm 25:4 aloud while others read the verse silently.
Let a second and a third volunteer read the verse aloud.

Read the words of "Teach Me Your Ways, O Lord," aloud and tell the students that this song is based on Psalm 25:4. The words of the song do not match the Bible verse words exactly, but they have the same meaning.

Say: Bible people—judges, kings, prophets, and ordinary people—needed to pray these words to God. We, too, need to pray these words. I will play the song again. Let's bow our heads in silent prayer as we listen to the song.

RESOURCES: Bibles, Cassette, cassette player, Class Pak Songbook

Amos: The Prophet of Justice

Seventeen books in the Old Testament are prophet books. God called prophets to speak God's message. Amos spoke God's message about justice (fairness).

Use a white crayon to write the words of Amos 5:24a in the space below. Then use watercolors to paint a picture in the space. God's message will appear in your picture.

Art: John Jordan

4-A

Life in CANAAN

The Old Testament includes twelve history books. Some of these books tell stories about judges and kings who were leaders of the Israelite people.

Use the Bible references to help you name some places where judges and kings served as leaders.

Deborah used to sit under the palm of Deborah between

_ _ _ _ _ _ and _ _ _ _ _ _ _

in the hill country of Ephraim; and the Israelites came up to her for judgment.
(Judges 4:4-5)

Art: John Jordan

Then Samuel said,

"Gather all Israel at _ _ _ _ _ _,
and I will pray to the LORD for you."

So they gathered at _ _ _ _ _ _,
. . . and said,
"We have sinned against the LORD."
And Samuel judged the people of Israel

at _ _ _ _ _ _.
(1 Samuel 7:5-6)

David was king of Israel for forty years:
he reigned seven years in

_ _ _ _ _ _ _,

and thirty-three years in

_ _ _ _ _ _ _ _ _ _.

(1 Kings 2:11)

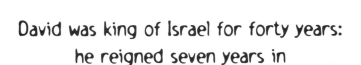

Art: John Jordan

4-B

Micah's Message

Micah is one of seventeen prophet books in our Bible. When Bible people forgot God's rules for living, God called prophets to speak God's message. Micah's words were an important message to Bible people. Micah's words are an important message to people today. Use the code to finish the computer screen message below. Check your work by reading the Bible reference.

He has told you, O MORTAL,

what is good; and what does the LORD

REQUIRE of you

but to do JUSTICE,

and to love KINDNESS,

and to WALK humbly with your God?

(MICAH 6:8)

Wise Words

Saul was Israel's first king.
David was Israel's second king.

To discover the name of Israel's third king
- Color spaces with a **v** **yellow**
- Color spaces with a **–** **blue**
- Color spaces with an **x** **red**

Israel's third king asked God to give him wisdom.
He grew so wise that people came from all nations to learn from him.

This third king wrote _____ proverbs and _____ songs.
(Read 1 Kings 4:32 to find how many proverbs and songs this king wrote.)

Use your Bible to complete these proverbs (wise sayings):

- A ___ ___ ___ ___ ___ ___ loves at all times. (Proverbs 17:17a)

- Train ___ ___ ___ ___ ___ ___ ___ ___ in the right way, and when old,
  they will not stray. (Proverbs 22:6)

4-D

Gospels: The Life of Jesus

Bible Passages

Matthew 2:1-11 - Wise men came to see Jesus.

Matthew 4:23 - Jesus taught and healed throughout Galilee.

Matthew 8:5-7 - Jesus promised to cure a centurion's servant.

Matthew 20:29-34 - Jesus healed two blind men.

Mark 16 - Jesus was raised from the dead.

Luke 2:1-16 - Shepherds came to see Jesus.

Luke 2:19 - Mary treasured these words in her heart.

Luke 2:39 - Jesus grew up in Nazareth.

John 6:3-14 - Jesus fed a multitude.

Children Will

- learn to find two parts of the story of Jesus' birth.
- learn to find the miracle of the feeding of the multitude.
- learn to find the Easter story.
- consider treasuring God's word in their hearts.

MARK YOUR BIBLE (10 minutes)

• Use Rainbow Ribbon Bookmarks

Before class write the following on the chalkboard:
Matthew 2 - yellow
Mark 16 - green
Luke 2 - blue

As the students arrive tell them to use the ribbons of their rainbow bookmarks (made in Session 1) to mark the Bible references. Tell them that Matthew, Mark, and Luke are the first three books in the New Testament. Encourage them to find the references without using the Table of Contents in their Bibles.

As students finish marking their Bibles, encourage them to begin work in the learning centers of their choice.

46

USE YOUR BIBLE (30 minutes)

Permission is granted to enlarge and display the instructions for the six learning center stations described in this section.

• The First Christmas (Art Center)

1. At Christmas, we celebrate the birth of Jesus our Savior. Follow instructions in "Jesus Is Born."

2. Draw a picture about Jesus' birth. You may use the star stickers to decorate the sky of your drawing.

Bibles, Reproducible 5A, pencils, paper, crayons or felt-tip markers, small gold or silver star stickers

• Sing Good News (Music Center)

Follow instructions in "Gospels."

RESOURCES: Bibles, Reproducible 5B, pencils, Cassette, cassette player

• Food and More (Food Center)

1. Follow instructions in "Miracle for a Multitude."

2. Eat twelve fish crackers.

RESOURCES: Bibles, Reproducible 5C, pencils, a basket of fish-shaped crackers

• Map It (Research Center)

1. Follow instructions in "Where Jesus Walked."

2. Can you find a map of Palestine in your Bible? If so, show it to a teacher.

RESOURCES: Bibles, Reproducible 5D, pencils

• <u>Play Bible Brain</u> (Game Center 1)

Play the game with others in this center. Directions are printed on the gameboard.

RESOURCES: Class Pak—pp. 11, 16 & 17

• <u>Play Bible Books</u> (Game Center 2)

Use the rules for Bible Books Game 1 (Old Testament/New Testament) to play this game with friends.

RESOURCES: Game cards from Class Pak—pp. 7 & 26, copy of game directions from page 87 in this book

RESPOND TO THE BIBLE MESSAGE
(20 minutes)

Ask the students to bring their Bibles and any reproducible sheets they completed to the gathering circle.

• <u>Find The Gospels</u>

Have everyone find Psalms by opening the Bible in the middle. Then have everyone find Matthew by opening the section held in the right hand at the middle. When everyone has found Matthew, have the students thumb through the pages to find Mark, then Luke, then John.

Say: The first four books in our New Testament are called "Gospels." They tell the story of Jesus. They tell about the birth of Jesus; they tell about the teachings of Jesus; they tell about the miracles of Jesus. They show us how much God loved the world— enough to send Jesus to the world.

Have the students find Mark 16 (which they marked earlier with the green ribbon of their bookmarks).

Continue: The gospels also tell us about the death and resurrection of Jesus. Jesus was killed on a cross, but God raised Jesus from the dead. That is good news. This good news is so important that all four Gospel books tell the story.

Show the students that Mark 16 tells the resurrection story. Many Bibles will have a subtitle and cross references under the subtitle, showing where the story can be found in the other three Gospels. If your students' Bibles offer this cross reference, let volunteers tell where the resurrection story can be found in Matthew (*28:1-10*) in Luke (*24:1-12*) and John (*20:1-10*)

Tell the students that the resurrection story is told a bit differently in each Gospel book. Tell them that early Christians told about the resurrection many years before the stories were written down. Help the children understand that, though the story details differ, the meaning of the stories is the same—God raised Jesus from the dead. God offers us new life through Jesus Christ.

RESOURCES: Bibles

• Review Learning Center Work

Use the following ideas to review some work done in learning centers:

1. Art Center: Let volunteers answer as you read Reproducible 5A aloud. Then let volunteers show the pictures they drew.

2. Music Center: Let volunteers answer as you read Reproducible 5B aloud.

3. Food Center: Let volunteers answer as you read Reproducible 5C aloud. Ask students why they think they were told to eat exactly twelve fish crackers? (*because after Jesus multiplied five loaves and two fish into a meal for 5,000, they had enough food left over to fill twelve baskets*)

4. Research Center: Let volunteers answer and show the location on the map as you read Reproducible 5D aloud.

5. Bible Brain Game: Ask a few questions from the game cards.

6. Bible Books Game: Hold up a few cards and let the children name that book as an Old Testament or New Testament book.

RESOURCES: Reproducible 5A, 5B, 5C, 5D; some game cards from Bible Brain Game and Bible Books Game

• Worship Together

Have the students find Luke 2 in their Bibles. Remind them Luke 2 tells about the birth of Jesus in Bethlehem, about angels singing to shepherds, and about the shepherds hurrying to Bethlehem to see the newborn baby.

Ask the students to read Luke 2:19 silently while you read the verse aloud.

Say: Mary, the mother of Jesus, heard the wonderful words being said about Jesus. Our Bible says she treasured the words and pondered (thought carefully about) them in her heart. For our closing prayer today, we will listen to the song "I Treasure Your Word." We will listen and think carefully. We will treasure God's word in our hearts.

Have the students bow their heads and close their eyes as you play the Cassette recording of "I Treasure Your Word."

RESOURCES: Bibles, Cassette, cassette player

Jesus Is Born

Our Bible has four gospel books:
Matthew, Mark, Luke, and John.
Two gospel books tell the story of Jesus' birth.

Read Matthew 2:1-11.
This gospel tells that ___ ___ ___ ___   ___ ___ ___

came to see Jesus, the king of the ___ ___ ___ ___.

Read Luke 2:1-16.
This gospel tells us that ___ ___ ___ ___ ___ ___ ___ ___ ___

came to see Jesus, who was born in ___ ___ ___ ___ ___ ___ ___ ___ ___.

5-A

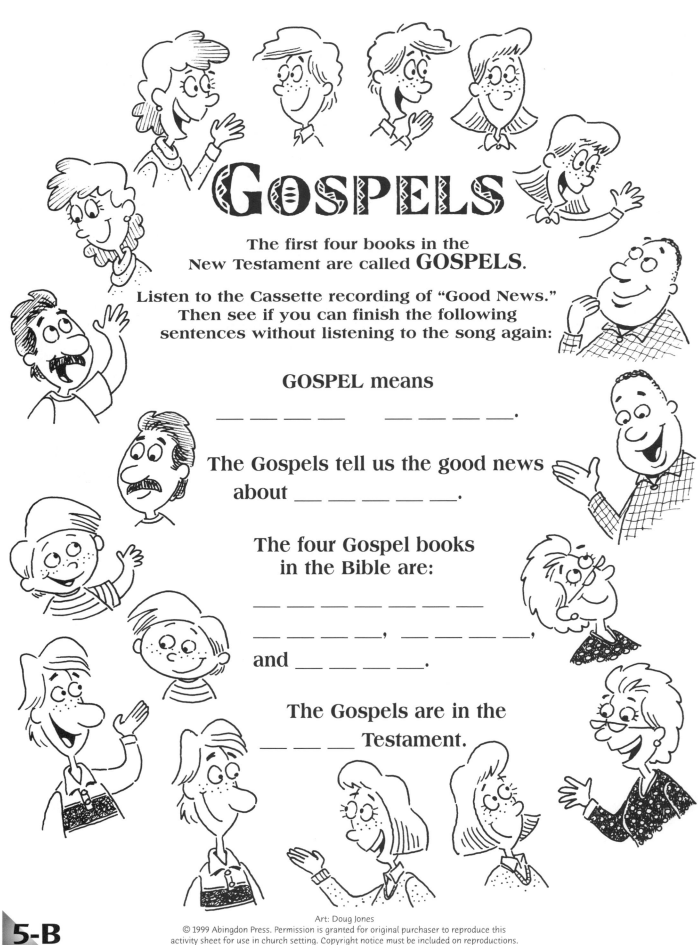

GOSPELS

The first four books in the
New Testament are called **GOSPELS**.

Listen to the Cassette recording of "Good News."
Then see if you can finish the following
sentences without listening to the song again:

GOSPEL means

— — — —   — — — —.

The Gospels tell us the good news
about __ __ __ __ __.

The four Gospel books
in the Bible are:

— — — — — — —

— — — —, — — — —,

and — — — —.

The Gospels are in the
— — — Testament.

miracle for a Multitude

Jesus came to show God's great love. Because Jesus loved people so much, he did many things to help them. Often Jesus helped in ways that astonished people. They could not understand how such wonderful things happened. We call these wonderful events "miracles." We know that miracles are a sign of God's presence.

One miracle story is told in all four Gospel Books of our Bible (Matthew, Mark, Luke, and John).

Read the story from John 6:3-14. Then use correct numbers to complete the sentences:

How many people offered a lunch to help Jesus feed the crowd?_____

How many fish were in the lunch?_____

How many loaves were in the lunch?_____

How many people were in the crowd? _____

How many baskets of food were left after everyone had eaten?_____

How many people were fed that day?_____

Art: John Jordan

Where Jesus Walked

Our Bible tells us that Jesus went about doing good. Use the Bible references to add the missing words. Then circle each place on the map of Palestine.

 1. When Jesus was born in

___ ___ ___ ___ ___ ___ ___ ___ ___

(Matthew 2:1), wise men from the East recognized Jesus as king of the Jews.

 2. Jesus grew up in the town of

___ ___ ___ ___ ___ ___ ___ ___

(Luke 2:39). Jesus grew and became strong, filled with wisdom; and the favor of God was upon him.

 3. When he grew up, Jesus traveled throughout

___ ___ ___ ___ ___ ___ ___

(Matthew 4:23), teaching and proclaiming the good news of the kingdom and curing every disease and every sickness among the people.

 4. At the town of

___ ___ ___ ___ ___ ___ ___ ___ ___

(Matthew 8:5-7), a centurion (Roman soldier) told Jesus that his servant was paralyzed. Jesus said, "I will come and cure him."

 5. Once when Jesus and his disciples were leaving

___ ___ ___ ___ ___ ___

(Matthew 20:29-34), two blind men asked Jesus to help them. Jesus touched their eyes. They regained their sight and followed Jesus.

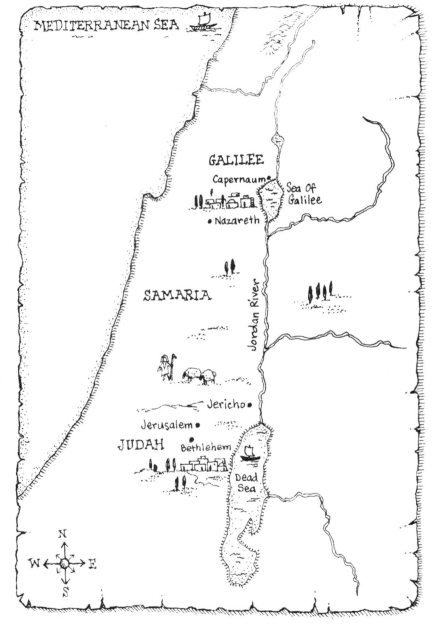

Map of Palestine: MEDITERRANEAN SEA, GALILEE, Capernaum, Sea Of Galilee, Nazareth, SAMARIA, Jordan River, Jericho, Jerusalem, JUDAH, Bethlehem, Dead Sea. Compass: N, S, E, W.

 5-D

Gospels: The Teachings of Jesus

Bible Passages

Matthew 5:16 -
Let your light shine.

Matthew 5:42 -
Give to others.

Matthew 5:44 -
Love your enemies.

Matthew 6:9-13 and
Luke 11:1-4 -
The Lord's Prayer

Matthew 6:14 -
Forgive others.

Matthew 6:21 -
Your heart will be where
your treasure is.

Matthew 7:7 -
Search and you will find.

Matthew 7:12 and
Luke 6:31 -
The Golden Rule

Matthew 7:24 -
Be like the wise man who
built a house on rock.

Matthew 22:36-39 -
The Great Commandment

Children Will
- realize that Jesus taught the disciples to pray.
- realize that Jesus taught the disciples to love God and love neighbor.
- realize that Jesus told stories to help people understand important ideas.

MARK YOUR BIBLE (5 minutes)

• Use Rainbow Ribbon Bookmarks

Before class write the following on the chalkboard:
Matthew 6 - yellow ribbon
Matthew 22 - green ribbon
Luke 6 - blue ribbon

As the students arrive tell them to use the ribbons of their rainbow bookmarks (made in Session 1) to mark the Bible references.

Remind them that Matthew and Luke are Gospel books. Encourage them to find the references without using the Table of Contents in their Bibles.

As students finish marking their Bibles, encourage them to begin work in the learning centers of their choice.

USE YOUR BIBLE (30 minutes)

Permission is granted to enlarge and display the instructions for the six learning center stations described in this section.

• <u>Make Prayer Baskets</u> (Art Center)

1. Follow instructions in "Let Us Pray" and in "Make a Prayer Basket.

2. Have you memorized "The Lord's Prayer"? If so, say the prayer with two friends.

RESOURCES: Bibles, Reproducible 6A, small paper bags, scissors, crayons or felt-tip markers, construction paper, pencils, stapler and staples

• <u>Sing the New Testament Books</u> (Music Center)

1. Find the Table of Contents in your Bible.

2. As you listen to the Cassette recording of "Books of the New Testament," read the names of the books from the Table of Contents in your Bible.

3. Then sing along with the Cassette recording.

RESOURCES: Bibles, Cassette, cassette player

• <u>The Cookie Question</u> (Food Center)

1. Follow instructions in "The Golden Rule."

2. Choose two cookies. If you follow the Golden Rule will you eat both cookies or will you give one to a friend?

RESOURCES: Bibles, pencils, Reproducible 6B, cookies (two per child)

• Complete the Crossword (Research Center)

Follow instructions in "Teachings of Jesus."

RESOURCES: Bibles, pencils, Reproducible 6C

• Play Bible Books (Game Center 1)

Use the rules of Bible Books Game 1 (Old Testament/New Testament) to play this game with friends.

RESOURCES: Game cards from Class Pak— pp. 7 & 26, copy of game directions from page 87 in this book

• Get Ready for Bible Bingo (Game Center 2)

1. Can you remember the names of some Old Testament Bible books?

2. Write the name of an Old Testament book on each square of "Bible Bingo Game Sheet."

3. Be sure to write your name on your paper.

4. Save the game sheet. We will use it later to play "Bible Bingo."

RESOURCES: Reproducible 6D, pencils

RESPOND TO THE BIBLE MESSAGE
(25 minutes)

Ask the students to bring their Bibles and any reproducible sheets they completed to the gathering circle.

• <u>Review Learning Center Work</u>

Use the following ideas to review some work done in learning centers:

1. Art Center: Remind the students that the Bible verses they read in this center almost match "The Lord's Prayer" we often pray in worship. Pray the prayer together. Encourage the children to take their prayer baskets home and use them as a reminder this week to pray about things that are important to them.

2. Music Center: Let a volunteer name the four Gospels (*Matthew, Mark, Luke, and John*). Let others name additional New Testament books. (Use the New Testament Library Poster to check their answers.)

3. Food Center: Let a volunteer read the "Golden Rule." Ask everyone who gave a cookie to a friend to raise his or her hand.

4. Bible Books Game: Hold up a few cards and let volunteers classify the books as Old Testament or New Testament.

RESOURCES:
Reproducible 6A, 6B, 6C; Class Pak—p. 5; some game cards from Bible Books Game

• <u>Play Bible Bingo</u>

Say: I will call out the names of Old Testament books. If you have that name on your paper, cross it out. When you have crossed off five names in a row, shout, "Bible Bingo!"

Call the names of the books at random. If the students seem interested, play the game until three players have shouted "Bible Bingo!"

Say: Today we have been learning things Jesus taught his followers. All those teachings are in the New Testament part of our Bible. Why do you think we played "Bible Bingo" using Old Testament books?

Help the children understand that the scriptures Jesus learned as a child were Old Testament scriptures. The New Testament was not written until many years after Jesus lived on earth.

Continue: Jesus knew the Old Testament scriptures. Jesus wanted to help people understand the Old Testament scriptures because they tell about God's love.

Explain: One day a lawyer asked Jesus which of God's commandments was the greatest. Jesus had learned the Ten Commandments. Jesus knew many other Bible verses about God's rules for living. Let's see how Jesus answered.

Have the students find Matthew 22:36-39 in their Bibles. Read the verses aloud while the students read silently.

Conclude: Jesus had learned the scriptures. Jesus had learned to understand the scriptures. Jesus knew that God's greatest rule was to love God and love neighbor.

RESOURCES: Bibles, Reproducible 6D, pencils

• Worship Together

Say: Jesus taught his followers to pray. He taught them to heal people. He taught them to love God and others. Sometimes Jesus told stories to help his followers understand. We call those stories parables. They are special stories that help us understand important ideas.

Continue: Those who learn Jesus' teachings and do them each day come to know Jesus in a special way. We, too, can follow Jesus.

Distribute Song Sheets (copied from page 9 of this book). Lead the children in singing "Teach Me Your Ways, O Lord" as a closing prayer.

RESOURCES: Cassette, cassette player, Song Sheets photocopied from page 9 in this book

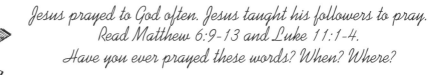

Jesus prayed to God often. Jesus taught his followers to pray.
Read Matthew 6:9-13 and Luke 11:1-4.
Have you ever prayed these words? When? Where?

God wants us to pray:
We can pray with spoken words. We can pray silently.
We can pray at church, at home, at school, in the car.
We can pray for many people. We can say
thank-you prayers, forgive-me prayers, and help-me prayers.

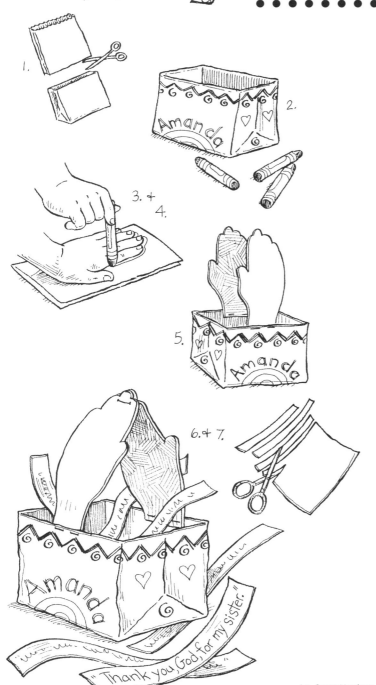

Make a Prayer Basket:

Supplies Needed:

small paper bag, scissors, crayons or felt-tip markers, construction paper, pencil, stapler and staples

Directions:

1. Cut the top half off a small paper bag. The bottom of the bag will be your prayer basket.

2. Decorate the sides of the bag with crayons or felt-tip markers. Write your name on the bag.

3. Fold a sheet of construction paper in half. With your fingers together, trace your hand on the paper.

4. Cut through both thicknesses of paper and you will have two hands.

5. Staple the wrist of one hand to each side of the basket.

6. Staple the fingertips of the paper hands together. The praying hands are the handle of your basket.

7. Cut the left-over part of the paper bag into slips. On one slip, write something you want to pray about. Place it in your basket.

6-A

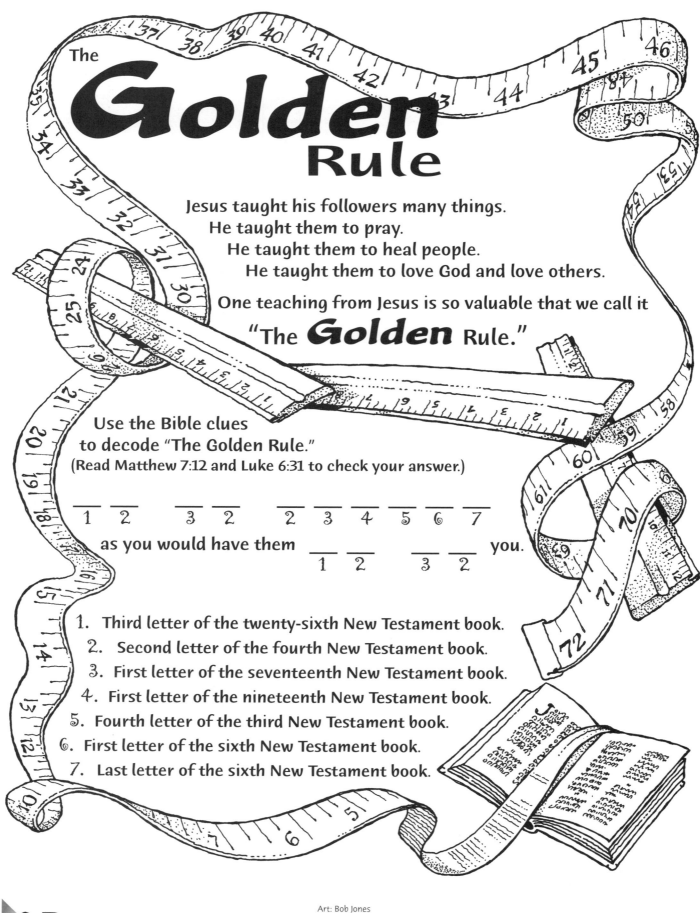

The Golden Rule

Jesus taught his followers many things.
He taught them to pray.
He taught them to heal people.
He taught them to love God and love others.

One teaching from Jesus is so valuable that we call it
"The Golden Rule."

Use the Bible clues
to decode "The Golden Rule."
(Read Matthew 7:12 and Luke 6:31 to check your answer.)

___ ___ ___ ___ ___ ___ ___ ___ ___ ___
1   2   3   2   2   3   4   5   6   7

as you would have them ___ ___ ___ ___ you.
                        1   2   3   2

1. Third letter of the twenty-sixth New Testament book.
2. Second letter of the fourth New Testament book.
3. First letter of the seventeenth New Testament book.
4. First letter of the nineteenth New Testament book.
5. Fourth letter of the third New Testament book.
6. First letter of the sixth New Testament book.
7. Last letter of the sixth New Testament book.

Teachings of Jesus

Jesus taught his followers that God's love is for all people, not just a few people. Jesus taught his followers to love all people, not just their friends.

Jesus taught his followers to forgive others. Jesus taught his followers to give to the poor, to care for the sick, and to be kind to visitors.

FOOD FOR POOR

Use your Bible to find the missing words and complete the crossword puzzle.

Across:

1. For where your
___ ___ ___ ___ ___ ___ ___ ___ is, there your heart will be also. (Matthew 6:21)

2. But I say to you, ___ ___ ___ ___ your enemies and pray for those who persecute you. (Matthew 5:44)

3. Give to everyone who begs from you, and do not ___ ___ ___ ___ ___ ___ anyone who wants to borrow from you. (Matthew 5:42)

Down:

1. For if you ___ ___ ___ ___ ___ ___ ___ others their trespasses, your heavenly Father will also forgive you. (Matthew 6:14)

2. Let your ___ ___ ___ ___ ___ shine before others, so that they may see your good works and give glory to your Father in heaven. (Matthew 5:16)

3. Ask, and it will be given you; ___ ___ ___ ___ ___ ___, and you will find; knock and the door will be opened for you. (Matthew 7:7)

4. Everyone then who hears these words of mine and acts on them will be like a ___ ___ ___ ___ man who built his house on rock. (Matthew 7:24)

Art: Bob Jones

Bible Bingo

free

6-D

7 Acts and New Testament Letters; Tell Good News

Children Will

- find information about the early church in the Book of Acts.

- find some teachings of the early church in the New Testament letters.

- recognize that God sent Jesus as Savior of the world.

MARK YOUR BIBLE (10 minutes)

• Use Rainbow Ribbon Bookmarks

Before class write the following on the chalkboard:
John 3 - yellow ribbon
Acts of the Apostles 2 - green ribbon
Romans 8 - blue ribbon

As the students arrive tell them to use the ribbons of their rainbow bookmarks (made in Session 1) to mark the Bible references.

Suggest that they first locate Matthew, then thumb forward to find the fourth Gospel book, John. Tell them that Acts of the Apostles comes after John. Then tell them that Romans comes after Acts. Encourage them to find the references without using the Table of Contents in their Bibles.

As students finish, ask them to find the Bible Dictionary/Concordance section in their Bibles. Ask them to find the definition of "apostle" (*one of the twelve disciples chosen by Jesus or certain early Christian leaders*). Then have them find the definition of "epistle" (*a letter, especially the letters included in the New Testament*). Tell the students they will be learning many things today about apostles and epistles (leaders and letters).

Then encourage students to begin work in the learning centers of their choice.

Bible Passages

John 3:16 -
God sent Jesus to save the world.

Acts 2:1-41 -
The story of Pentecost

Acts 3:1 -
Peter and John went to pray at the temple.

Acts 6:8 -
Stephen did great wonders and signs.

Acts 8:5 -
Philip preached in Samaria.

Acts 9:36 -
Dorcas was devoted to acts of charity.

Acts 12:12 -
Peter, released from prison, went to Mary's house, where many had gathered for prayer.

Acts 15:36 -
Paul and Barnabas visited churches they had established.

Romans 8:14, 28 -
God's children are led by God's Spirit; all things work for good for those who love God.

1 Corinthians 3:16 -
God's Spirit dwells in you.

Philippians 1:3 -
I thank God when I remember you.

1 John 4:7 -
Let us love one another; love is from God.

Permission is granted to enlarge and display the instructions for the six learning center stations described in this section.

• Make a Pentecost Candle (Art Center)

Follow instructions in "The Church Is Born" and "Make a Pentecost Candle."

RESOURCES: Bibles; Reproducible 7A; pencils; votive candles; red, yellow, and orange tissue paper; scissors; paint brushes; white glue thinned with water

• Sing "Apostles and Epistles" (Music Center)

Use the Songbook and the Cassette to sing "Apostles and Epistles."

RESOURCES: Cassette, cassette player, Class Pak Songbook.

• Food for Thought (Food Center)

1. Follow instructions in "Good Words from New Testament Letters."

2. Decide which Bible verse you like best. Read that verse's missing good word.

3. Use raisins to spell your favorite verse's missing good word on your napkin.

4. As you eat your raisins, try to memorize your favorite verse.

RESOURCES: Bibles, Reproducible 7B, pencils, raisins, napkins

- ## Crack the Code (Research Center 1)

Follow instructions in "Some Early Christian Leaders."

RESOURCES: Bibles, Reproducible 7C, pencils

- ## Work a Perfect Square (Research Center 2)

Follow instructions in "The Good News Spreads."

RESOURCES: Bibles, Reproducible 7D, pencils

- ## Play Bible Books Game (Game Center)

1. Work with friends.

2. Read the names of the New Testament Books from the New Testament Library Poster.

3. Then, see if everyone can work together to arrange the New Testament Bible Books Game Cards in the correct order.

RESOURCES: Display the New Testament Library (Class Pak—p. 5), provide the New Testament cards (40-66) from Bible Books Game (Class Pak—pp. 7 & 26). NOTE: If students need help, suggest that they divide the task by letting each member of the group learn the order of a few books.

RESPOND TO THE BIBLE MESSAGE
(20 minutes)

Ask the students to bring their Bibles and any reproducible sheets they completed to the gathering circle.

• Find Some Bible Books

Demonstrating with your own Bible, lead the children in following instructions 1-8 on Class Pak—p. 28 to find Psalms, Deuteronomy, Matthew, and Romans. Be sure to include this poster's information about the type books they are holding in left hands and right hands.

Then have the students thumb back a few pages to find the Book of Acts. Let a volunteer tell the complete title of this book (*The Acts of the Apostles*).

Say: **This book is about the acts/actions of Jesus' followers. This books is about the beginning of the Christian church. After Jesus returned to God, his disciples—also called apostles—continued his ministry. Through the teachings of the disciples, others came to know and accept Jesus as the Christ.**

Explain: **Christ means anointed one. As Christians we believe that Jesus was sent by God and chosen by God to help us know God in a special way.**

Continue: **As the early disciples told the good news of Jesus Christ, others believed what they were saying. They, too, became disciples. These early followers of Jesus met every day to eat together, to pray for each other, and to worship God. These meetings were the beginning of the church.**

Conclude: **The church is not just a building. *Church* means all the people everywhere who follow Jesus. We are a part of the church. We continue to carry on Jesus' ministry.**

RESOURCES: Bibles, Class Pak—p. 28

• Review Learning Center Work

Use the following ideas to review some work done in learning centers:

1. Art Center: Let volunteers answer as you read Reproducible 7A aloud. Then let volunteers show their Pentecost Candles.

2. Music Center: Let volunteers explain the difference between an apostle (*a leader in the early church*) and an epistle (*a letter written by leaders in the early church to help Christians remain faithful*).

3. Food Center: Let volunteers answer as you read Reproducible 7B aloud. Ask what words they spelled with their raisins.

4. Crack the Code Center: Let volunteers answer as you read Reproducible 7C aloud.

5. Work a Perfect Square Center: Let volunteers answer as you read Reproducible 7D aloud. As answers are read let volunteers find Galatia, Rome, Philippi, and Thessalonica on the Map: Into All the World (Class Pak—pp. 13 & 20).

6. Bible Books Center: Ask if any group working in this center was able to arrange the New Testament Books in the correct order without looking. If so, let them tell what methods they used (*for instance, each group member memorizing the order of five books*).

RESOURCES: Reproducible 7A, 7B, 7C, 7D; Class Pak—pp. 13 & 20

• Worship Together

Have the students find John 3:16 in their Bibles. Lead them in reading this verse in unison.

Say: Our Bible is filled with stories of God's love for people. Because God loves the people of the whole world, God sent Jesus, our Savior.

Continue: As we read our Bibles, we learn more about God's great power and about Jesus' amazing love for us. Our God is awesome.

Hand out Song Sheets (photocopied from page 9 in this book). Using the Cassette for accompaniment, lead the students in singing "The Heavens Tell God's Glory."

Close with prayer, asking God to help members of your class remain faithful in reading their Bibles and in continuing the ministry of Jesus.

RESOURCES: Bibles, Cassette, Song Sheets copied from page 9 in this book

The Church Is Born

After Jesus rose from the dead, he told his followers to go into all the world. They were to preach, baptize, and teach all that Jesus had taught them. Jesus promised to be with them in this work. Jesus promised to send the Holy Spirit to help them with their work.

Use the Bible clues to finish the story:

- Soon after Jesus returned to God, his followers were all gathered in one place in Jerusalem to celebrate the spring harvest festival day of __ __ __ __ __ __ __ __ __ __ (Acts 2:1).

- Suddenly the room where they were gathered was filled with a sound like the rush of a violent __ __ __ __ (Acts 2:2). Then tongues of __ __ __ __ (Acts 2:3) appeared. All were filled with the __ __ __ __ __ __ __ __ __ __ (Acts 2:4) and began to speak in other languages.

- Jews from many nations were living in Jerusalem. When they heard the followers of Jesus speaking, a crowd gathered. Everyone was bewildered, because each one heard them speaking in the native __ __ __ __ __ __ __ __ of each (Acts 2:6).

- Peter preached that day, telling everyone about Jesus. That day about __ __ __ __ __   __ __ __ __ __ __ __ __ people were baptized and added as followers of Jesus. (Acts 2:41)

We call the day this happened the day of Pentecost. We call it the birthday of the church.

Make a Pentecost Candle

Supplies:
a votive candle; red, yellow, and orange tissue paper; scissors; a paint brush; white glue thinned with water

Directions:
1. Cut the tissue paper into small pieces.
2. Hold each piece of tissue paper against the side of the candle and paint over it with glue.
3. Overlap the pieces to get additional colors.

7-A

Good Words from New Testament Letters

Twenty-two books in our New Testament are letters. Some early Christian leaders wrote letters to help others become faithful followers of Jesus.

Some New Testament letters are named for the town or area they were first addressed to. Some letters are named for the person they were sent to. Some letters are named for the person writing the letter. Write the missing good word on each scroll to learn a teaching from one of the New Testament letters.

For all who are _____ by the Spirit of God are children of God.
(Romans 8:14)

We know that all things work together for _____ for those who love God.
(Romans 8:28)

Do you not know that you are God's temple and that God's _____ dwells in you?
(1 Corinthians 3:16)

I _____ my God every time I remember you. (Philippians 1:3)

Beloved, let us _____ one another; because love is from God.
(1 John 4:7)

Art: John Jordan

Some Early Christian Leaders

A	B	C
• · / · ·	• · / • ·	• • / · ·
D	E	F
• • / · •	• · / · •	• • / · •
G	H	I
• • / • •	• · / • ·	· • / • ·
J	K	L
· • / • •	• · / · · / • ·	• · / • · / • ·
M	N	O
• • / · · / • ·	• • / · • / • ·	• · / · • / • ·
P	Q	R
• • / • • / • ·	• • / • • / · •	• • / · • / • ·
S	T	U
· • / • · / • ·	· • / • • / · ·	• · / · · / • •
V	W	X
• · / • · / • •	· • / • • / · •	• • / · · / • •
Y	Z	
• • / · • / • •	• · / · • / • •	

After Jesus returned to God, his followers carried on his work. They taught others what Jesus had said. They healed people in the name of Jesus. They told others how Jesus had shown them what God is like. Soon followers of Jesus Christ were called Christians.

Some of the men and women who became Christians are named in the book called The Acts of the Apostles. Use the Braille code to learn the names of some of these first Christians. Then read the Bible references to see if you decoded the names correctly.

⠠ ⠠ ⠠ ⠠ ⠠

__ __ __ __ __ said to them, "Repent, and be baptized every one of you in the name of Jesus Christ..." (Acts 2:38)

⠠ ⠠ ⠠ ⠠

One day Peter and __ __ __ __ were going up to the temple at the hour of prayer. (Acts 3:1)

⠠ ⠠ ⠠ ⠠ ⠠ ⠠ ⠠

__ __ __ __ __ __ __, full of grace and power, did great wonders and signs among the people. (Acts 6:8)

⠠ ⠠ ⠠ ⠠ ⠠ ⠠

__ __ __ __ __ __ went down to the city of Samaria and proclaimed the Messiah to them. (Acts 8:5)

Now in Joppa there was a disciple whose name was Tabitha,

⠠ ⠠ ⠠ ⠠ ⠠ ⠠

which in Greek is __ __ __ __ __ __. She was devoted to good works and acts of charity. (Acts 9:36)

As soon as he realized this, he went to the house of

⠠ ⠠ ⠠ ⠠

__ __ __ __, the mother of John...where many had gathered and were praying. (Acts 12:12)

⠠ ⠠ ⠠ ⠠

After some days __ __ __ __ said to

⠠ ⠠ ⠠ ⠠ ⠠ ⠠ ⠠

__ __ __ __ __ __ __ __, "Come let us return and visit the believers in every city where we proclaimed the word of the Lord and see how they are doing." (Acts 15:36)

The Good News Spreads

The twenty-seven books of the New Testament tell about Jesus and about those who told the story of Jesus to others. Choose the numbered statement that matches each word. Write the number in the proper square. When all your answers are correct, the numbers will total 15 across each row and down each column.

Peanut Butter

1. This letter was written to the churches of Galatia.

2. This book tells about the actions of the apostles.

3. This word means "good news."

4. This book is one of the four Gospels in the New Testament.

5. This letter was written to Christians living in Rome.

Jelly

6. This letter was written to Christians at Philippi.

7. Four New Testament books have this name in their titles.

8. Two New Testament letters were written to this man.

9. This New Testament letter was written to Christians of Thessalonica.

.

8 *A Treasure Book for Everyone*

Bible Passages

Deuteronomy 6:5 -
Love God with all
your heart.

Matthew 18:20 -
Where two are gathered
in the name of Jesus,
Christ is there.

Matthew 28:18-20 -
Go into all the world.

Mark 12:28-31 -
The Great Commandment

Children Will
- learn that many inventions made it possible for the Bible to be written and copied.
- realize that Christians have taken the Bible into many lands as they told others the good news of Jesus.

MARK YOUR BIBLE (10 minutes)

• Use Rainbow Ribbon Bookmarks

Before class write the following on the chalkboard:
Deuteronomy 6 - yellow ribbon
Matthew 28 - green ribbon
Mark 12 - blue ribbon

As the students arrive tell them to use the ribbons of their rainbow bookmarks (made in Session 1) to mark the Bible references. Encourage them to help each other.

As the students finish marking their Bible references, call attention to the Timeline: "The Bible, A Book for All Times" (Class Pak—pp. 15 & 18). Help the children find the years when Jesus lived on earth on this timeline.

Show them that the years before Jesus lived are written as "B.C." (before Christ) on this timeline and that the B.C. years are counted backward.

Show them that the years after Jesus was born are written as "A.D." (for the Latin words *anno Domini,* which mean "in the year of our Lord"). Let them find the place on the timeline that approximates this year.

RESOURCES: Bibles, rainbow ribbon bookmarks made in session 1, chalkboard and chalk

Say: The stories and teachings of our Bible have been told for thousands of years. Today we will discover how the Bible message spread to many lands and into many languages.

Continue: Hold your Bible in your hand. The Bible message is a gift to you from God. The Bible in your hand is also a gift to you from many people. Several things had to be invented before the Bible in your hand was possible. It took many years and many people to give this gift to you.

Tell the students they can discover ways the Bible message spread as they work in today's learning centers. Remind them that they may work in centers for 30 minutes and that they should complete all the activities in one center before moving to another center.

RESOURCES: Bibles, rainbow ribbon bookmarks (made in Session 1), Class Pak—pp. 15 & 18

USE YOUR BIBLE (30 minutes)

Permission is granted to enlarge and display the instructions for the five learning center stations described in this section.

• Make a Scroll (Art Center)

1. Follow instructions in "Great Inventions" and in "Make a Scroll."
2. Then read Mark 12:28-31 from your Bible. Do some of the words from Mark match the words from Deuteronomy you wrote on your scroll?

RESOURCES: Bibles; Reproducible 8A, 8B; pencils, lunch-size paper bags; felt-tip markers; tape; straws; yarn

• Sing "Wonderful Book" (Music Center)

1. Follow instructions in "How the Bible Began."

2. Read Matthew 18:20 in your Bible.

3. Then sing "Wonderful Book of God's People" with two friends. Share the Songbook. Use the Cassette to accompany your singing.

RESOURCES: Bibles, Reproducible 8C, pencils, Class Pak Songbook, Cassette, cassette player

• Enjoy Bread (Food Center)

1. Follow instructions in "One Book, Many Languages."

2. Read Matthew 28:18-20 in your Bible.

3. People in different countries speak different languages. They also eat different kinds of bread. Choose two kinds of bread to eat.

4. As you eat your bread, thank God for Christians who have helped translate our Bible into almost 2,000 languages.

RESOURCES: Bibles, Reproducible 8D, pencils, breads from several traditions—such as tortillas, pita bread, crackers, pretzels, and wheat bread

• Use a Timeline (Research Center)

Work with friends to attach the cards in the correct places on the Timeline, "The Bible: A Book for All Times."

RESOURCES: Class Pak—pp. 15 & 18, 23; push pins or loops of tape for attaching the cards

• Play Bible Books (Game Center)

Use the rules for Bible Books Game 3 to play this game with friends.

RESOURCES: Game cards from Class Pak— pp. 7 & 26, game directions copied from page 87 in this book

RESPOND TO THE BIBLE MESSAGE
(20 minutes)

Ask the students to bring their Bibles and any reproducible sheets they completed to the gathering circle.

• Review Learning Center Work

Display the Map: "Into All the World" (Class Pak—pp. 13 & 20) and the Timeline: "The Bible: A Book for All Times" (Class Pak—pp. 15 & 18). Use the following ideas to review work done in learning centers:

1. Art Center: Let volunteers answer as you read "Great Inventions" (from Reproducible 8A) aloud. Using the Class Pak Map: "Into All the World," let volunteers find Egypt (where papyrus reeds were made into sheets for writing), Rome (where Romans invented codex books), China (where paper was invented), and Germany (where Gutenberg invented the printing press).

2. Music Center: Let volunteers answer as you read Reproducible 8C aloud. Let volunteers sing "Wonderful Book of God's People."

3. Food Center: Let volunteers answer as you read Reproducible 8D aloud. Using the Class Pak Map: "Into All the World," let volunteers find the Holy Land (where people began to write down the Old Testament stories in Hebrew and the New Testament stories in Greek). Let other volunteers use the map to find Rome (where Jerome translated the New Testament from Greek to Latin) and Bethlehem (where Jerome translated the Old Testament from Hebrew to Latin). Let additional volunteers use the map to locate England (where John Wycliffe and others translated the Bible into English), Germany (where Martin Luther translated the Bible into German), and India (because William Carey translated parts of the Bible into forty languages for the people of India).

4. Research Center: Let volunteers read the cards they added to the timeline.

5. Bible Books Game: Ask how difficult it was to put all 66 cards in the correct order.

RESOURCES: Reproducible 8A, 8C, 8D; Class Pak—pp. 13 & 20, 15 & 18, 23; Cassette; cassette player

• Worship Together

Have students find Matthew 28:18-20 in their Bibles. Let a volunteer read the verses aloud as others read silently.

Point to Galilee on the map.

Say: Jesus told his followers to go into all the world to preach, to baptize, and to teach. They obeyed, and the good news of Jesus spread from town to town, from country to country, and from continent to continent.

Continue: We know that soon after Jesus died, Philip told the good news to a man from Africa. Soon, many of the people in North Africa were Christians. (Point to North Africa on the map.) We know that Paul and his companions traveled as far as Rome to start new churches. (Point to Galatia, Philippi, and Rome on the map.)

Conclude: For hundreds of years, Christians have carried the Bible with them as they traveled to other countries to tell the good news of Jesus. As we have learned today, it took thousands of years and the inventions of many people to make it possible for Bibles to be read in almost 2,000 languages and in hundreds of countries.

Ask the students to hold their unopened Bibles in their hands.

Say: The Bible message is a gift to you from God. The Bible in your hand is also a gift to you from many people. It took many inventions, many years, and many people to give this gift to you.

Remind the children that the Bible contains much more than they have been able to learn in the past eight sessions. Remind them that using the Bible is a lifelong activity.

Give each student a copy of Reproducible 8E. Tell them to fold this paper, place it in their Bibles, and use it as a guide as they continue to read and learn from their Bibles.

Say: The more you read your Bible, the more you will learn to treasure God's word in your heart.

Hand out Song Sheets (photocopied from page 9 in this book). Using the Cassette for accompaniment, lead the students in singing "I Treasure Your Word" for your closing prayer.

RESOURCES: Bibles, Class Pak—pp. 13 & 20, Reproducible 8E, Song Sheets photocopied from page 9 in this book, Cassette, cassette player

Great Inventions

1	=	A
2	=	B
3	=	C
4	=	D
5	=	E
6	=	F
7	=	G
8	=	H
9	=	I
10	=	J
11	=	K
12	=	L
13	=	M
14	=	N
15	=	O
16	=	P
17	=	Q
18	=	R
19	=	S
20	=	T
21	=	U
22	=	V
23	=	W
24	=	X
25	=	Y
26	=	Z

Use the number/alphabet code to finish the story:

Long ago people did not know how to write. The stories and teachings of the Bible were told for many years before they were written down.

When people began to invent writing, they made pictures to tell a story.
They invented ___ ___ ___ ___ ___ ___ ___   ___ ___ ___ ___ ___ ___ ___
16 9 3 20 21 18 5   23 18 9 20 9 14 7

Each word had a different picture or sign.
Writing this way was slow.

About 1700 B.C. people began to invent

___ ___ ___ ___ ___ ___ ___ ___ ___. Now many words could
1 12 16 8 1 2 5 20 19

be made using only a few signs (or letters). The Hebrews (Bible people) developed an alphabet. After this, they began to write down some of the stories and songs included in the Old Testament portion of our Bible.

The invention of writing was wonderful. But it was important to have things to write on. People carved their writings on clay. They used vegetable dyes to write on wood.

Art: Doug Jones

About 3000 B.C. the people in Egypt learned to make

___ ___ ___ ___ ___ ___ ___, a writing surface a bit
16 1   16 25 18 21 19

like paper. They cut the papyrus reeds that grew in marshes into thin strips, then pressed the strips into sheets.

People also began to soak animal skins in lime water, scrape the hair off, and stretch the skins tight to make

___ ___ ___ ___ ___ ___ ___ ___ ___. These skins were
16 1   18 3   8   13 5   14 20

cut into pieces and fastened together in long strips. The strips were rolled into scrolls. Papyrus was also made into scrolls. We believe most books of the Bible were first written

on ___ ___ ___ ___ ___ ___ ___.
   19 3   18 15 12 12 19

About A.D. 100 the Romans got the idea of sewing parchment sheets together at the middle and folding them, like the books we have today. These early books were called

___ ___ ___ ___ ___ ___ ___ ___ ___ ___.
3   15 4   5   24   2   15 15 11 19

For more than 3,000 years after people learned to write, there was only one way to make copies of a scroll or book. Each had to be copied by hand.

Around A.D. 1450 Johann Gutenberg invented the

___ ___ ___ ___ ___ ___ ___ ___ ___ ___ ___ ___ ___.
16 18 9   14 20 9   14 7   16 18 5   19 19

Now many copies of books could be made at one time, and all the copies would be alike.

Copies could be made on ___ ___ ___ ___ ___, which had
                         16 1   16 5   18

been invented by the Chinese about 1600 years before. One of the first books Gutenberg printed

was a ___ ___ ___ ___ ___.
      2   9   2   12 5

8-A

Make a Scroll

Supplies

a lunch size paper bag
two straws
tape
yarn
a felt-tip marker

Directions

1. Tear the bottom from the paper bag.

2. Tear the bag open at the seam.

3. Crumple the bag in your hands. Then smooth it out.

4. Repeat crumpling and smoothing the bag until your paper looks a bit like an animal skin.

5. Write the words of Deuteronomy 6:5 on your paper. Be sure to include the Bible reference.

You shall love the LORD your God with all your heart, and with all your soul, and with all your might.
Deuteronomy 6:5

6. Tape a straw to each end of your paper.

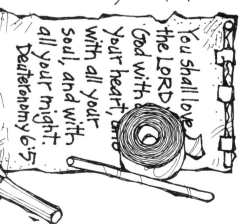

You shall love the LORD your God with all your heart, and with all your soul, and with all your might.
Deuteronomy 6:5

7. Roll the paper into a scroll and tie it with yarn.

Art: Brenda Gilliam

8-B

1	=	A
2	=	B
3	=	C
4	=	D
5	=	E
6	=	F
7	=	G
8	=	H
9	=	I
10	=	J
11	=	K
12	=	L
13	=	M
14	=	N
15	=	O
16	=	P
17	=	Q
18	=	R
19	=	S
20	=	T
21	=	U
22	=	V
23	=	W
24	=	X
25	=	Y
26	=	Z

How Our Bible Began

Use the number/alphabet code to finish the story:

Long ago there were no written Bible stories. The people told the stories from memory. Parents told them to their children, who told them to their children. They did not read them, because the Bible had not been written. We call this word of mouth telling of the Bible stories and

teachings ___ ___ ___ ___   ___ ___ ___ ___ ___ ___ ___ ___ ___ .
         15 18 1 12   20 18 1 4 9 20 9 15 14

(meaning mouth)   (meaning something done again and again)

The stories and teachings of the ___ ___ ___   ___ ___ ___ ___ ___ ___ ___ ___ ___
                                  15 12 4   20 5 19 20 1 13 5 14 20

were told for hundreds of years before they were written. About 950 B.C. Bible people began to write down some of the Old Testament stories.

The stories and teachings of the ___ ___ ___   ___ ___ ___ ___ ___ ___ ___ ___ ___ were told
                                 14 5 23   20 5 19 20 1 13 5 14 20

for many years before they were written. Some of the New Testament ___ ___ ___ ___ ___ ___ ___
                                                                    12 5 20 20 5 18 19

were written about twenty-five years after Jesus died. Then, about thirty years after Jesus died,
people began to write down the stories and teachings of Jesus that are included in

the four ___ ___ ___ ___ ___ ___ Books—Matthew, Mark, Luke, and John.
         7 15 19 16 5 12

It took many people and more than 1,000 years for the stories, songs, and messages of the Bible to

be ___ ___ ___ ___ ___ ___ ___ .
   23 18 9 20 20 5 14

8-C

One Book...Many Languages

Use the number/alphabet code to complete the following:

1 = A	8 = H	15 = O	22 = V
2 = B	9 = I	16 = P	23 = W
3 = C	10 = J	17 = Q	24 = X
4 = D	11 = K	18 = R	25 = Y
5 = E	12 = L	19 = S	26 = Z
6 = F	13 = M	20 = T	
7 = G	14 = N	21 = U	

The Hebrews (Bible people) began to write down the stories and teachings of the Old Testament about 3,000 years ago. They wrote the Old Testament in the language they spoke. That language was

___ ___ ___ ___ ___ ___.
8   5   2   18 5   23

After a while many Hebrews moved away from the land of Judah to other countries. No longer were they called Hebrews. They were called Jews. They lived in North Africa, in Italy, in Greece, in India. Many forgot how to read or speak Hebrew. They learned to speak other languages.

By the time all the Old Testament books were written, the Greeks were the most powerful people in the part of the world where Bible people lived. Many languages were used in this part of the world, but the

___ ___ ___ ___ ___ language was used almost everywhere
7   18 5   5   11
people went.

So Jewish scholars translated (changed) the holy scriptures of the Old Testament from ___ ___ ___ ___ ___ ___ to
8   5   2   18 5   23

___ ___ ___ ___ ___. Now the holy books of the Old Testament
7   18 5   5   11
could be read in two languages.

By the time Jesus lived, Jewish people who lived in Bible lands spoke Aramaic. But, the followers of Jesus knew that the good news of Jesus was for everyone. Most people also spoke Greek. So the books of the

New Testament were first written in ___ ___ ___ ___ ___.
7   18 5   5   11

Later, many people began to speak Latin. A man named Jerome worked more than twenty years to translate (change) the Bible into

___ ___ ___ ___ ___. While living in Rome Jerome translated the
12 1   20 9   14
New Testament from its original language, ___ ___ ___ ___ ___.
7   18 5   5   11
Then Jerome moved to Bethlehem, where he translated the Old

Testament from its original language, ___ ___ ___ ___ ___ ___.
8   5   2   18 5   23

Christians carried the good news of Jesus to many countries. They carried Bibles with them. People in other countries needed to be able to read the Bible in their own languages. John Wycliffe led the group that first

translated the Bible into the ___ ___ ___ ___ ___ ___ ___
5   14 7   12 9   19 8
language. Martin Luther translated the Bible into

___ ___ ___ ___ ___ ___. William Carey translated parts of the
7   5   18 13 1   14
Bible into forty languages for the people of ___ ___ ___ ___ ___.
9   14 4   9   1

The Bible has been translated into almost 2,000

___ ___ ___ ___ ___ ___ ___ ___ ___.
12 1   14 7   21 1   7   5   19

8-D

More Treasures

Our Bible is a book of treasures.

No one has ever completed studying the Bible and finding the Bible's treasures. Fold this paper and place it in your Bible. Check the boxes as you read the stories.

Parables of Jesus

❏ The sower (Mark 4:3-9)

❏ The good Samaritan (Luke 10:25-37)

❏ The lost sheep (Luke 15:4-7)

❏ The two debtors (Luke 7:41-43)

❏ The rich fool (Luke 12:16-21)

❏ The lost coin (Luke 15:8-10)

❏ The great banquet (Matthew 22:1-10)

❏ The laborers in the vineyard (Matthew 20:1-16)

❏ The prodigal son (Luke 15:11-32)

❏ The ten bridesmaids (Matthew 25:1-13)

Miracles of Jesus

❏ Feeding the multitude (John 6:1-14)

❏ Walking on the water (Matthew 14:22-33)

❏ Turning water into wine (John 2:1-11)

❏ Casting out demons (Luke 8:26-33)

❏ Healing the blind man (John 9:1-41)

❏ Raising of Lazarus (John 11:1-44)

❏ Raising Jarius' daughter (Mark 5:21-43)

❏ Healing the paralytic (Mark 2:1-12)

❏ Healing a leper (Matthew 8:1-4)

❏ Healing a centurion's servant (Luke 7:1-10)

Acts of the Apostles

❏ Peter and John heal at the Temple (Acts 3:1-10)

❏ Philip and the man from Ethiopia (Acts 8:26-39)

❏ Saul's conversion (Acts 9:1-19)

❏ Peter and Cornelius (Acts 10)

❏ Peter rescued from prison (Acts 12:6-17)

Old Testament Stories

❏ The first Creation story (Genesis 1:1–2:4a)

❏ The second Creation story (Genesis (2:4b-25)

❏ The Flood (Genesis 6:5–8:22)

❏ The call of Abram (Abraham) (Genesis 12:1-5a)

❏ Jacob's ladder (Genesis 28:10-17)

❏ Joseph's special robe (Genesis 37:1-36)

❏ Moses and the burning bush (Exodus 3:1-22)

❏ The Passover (Exodus 11:1–12:51)

❏ The Exodus (parting of the sea) (Exodus 14:1-31)

❏ Joshua and the battle of Jericho (Joshua 6:1-20)

❏ Call of Samuel (1 Samuel 3:1-20)

❏ Anointing of David (1 Samuel 16:1-13)

❏ David and Goliath (1 Samuel 17:1-54)

❏ Elijah and the prophets of Baal (1 Kings 18:20-39)

❏ Isaiah's vision (Isaiah 6:1-8)

❏ The fiery furnace (Daniel 3:1-28)

❏ Daniel in the lions' den (Daniel 6:1-23)

❏ Jonah and the large fish (Jonah 1:1–3:10)

Games

Game Directions: Bible Books

Rules for Game 1

1. Shuffle the 66 cards, then place them in rows, rainbow side up.
2. Decide who will play first. Play continues clockwise.
3. When it is your turn, choose a card and read the name of the book aloud.
4. Tell whether the book is in the Old Testament or the New Testament. (Check answer by reading the back of the card).
5. If your answer is correct, keep the card. If your answer is incorrect, return the card to play.
6. When all cards have been claimed, the player holding the most cards wins.

Rules for Game 2

1. Shuffle the 66 cards, then place them in rows, rainbow side up.
2. Decide who will play first. Play continues clockwise.
3. When it is your turn, choose a card and read the name of the book aloud.
4. Tell what kind of literature the book is (law, history, poetry and song, prophet, gospel, letter).
5. If your answer is correct, keep the card. If your answer is incorrect, return the card to play.
6. When all cards have been claimed, the player holding the most cards wins.

Rules for Game 3

Work with friends to place the books in the correct order—39 books in the Old Testament and 27 books in the New Testament.

Hint: If you divide the books into literature groups first (law, history, poetry and song, prophet, gospel, letter) you will be able to work faster.

Games

GAME DIRECTIONS: BIBLE TOSS

Get Ready

1. Cut out the gameboard on Class Pak—p. 9.
2. Fold the gameboard on the broken lines toward the front of the board. Tape the corner tabs to form a vertical lid. This will keep the playing pieces from falling off the board.
3. Cut out the game cards on Class Pak—p. 22.
4. Shuffle the cards and stack them beside the board.
5. Give each player a marker (coin, button, small pebble) and a piece of paper and a pencil for tallying his or her score.

Play

Sit in a circle around the gameboard. Players take turns doing the following:

1. Toss a marker on the gameboard.
2. Add the indicated points (written in the space on the gameboard on which the marker falls) to the tally sheet.
3. Draw a game card, read the question, and answer it. If the answer is correct, keep the points. If the answer is incorrect, subtract the points from the tally sheet.

Continue playing clockwise until all cards have been drawn. The player with the most points wins.

Learning To Use My Bible

Answers to Reproducible Pages

• Reproducible 1B, "Find Hidden Treasures"

You have put **GLADNESS** in my heart.
I will give **THANKS** to the LORD with my whole heart.
Create in me a **CLEAN** heart, O God.
I **TREASURE** your word in my heart.

• Reproducible 2A, "Bible Library"

39 books are in the Old Testament
27 books are in the New Testament
66 books are in the Bible

• Reproducible 2B, "Return the Books"

Exodus
Ruth
2 Kings
Ezra
Psalms
Amos
Micah
Mark
Romans
Galatians
Ephesians
Titus
Jude

• Reproducible 2C, "Most Popular Book"

The Old Testament was first written in the **HEBREW** language.
The New Testament was first written in the **GREEK** language.
Over the years the Bible has been translated into almost **TWO THOUSAND** languages.

Reproducible 3A, "God's Mighty Acts: Creation"

In the beginning . . . God created the **HEAVENS** and the **EARTH**.

Reproducible 3B, "Manna and More"

You shall have no other **GODS** before me. (verse 3)
You shall not make for yourself an **IDOL**. (verse 4)
You shall not make wrongful use of the **NAME** of the LORD. (verse 7)
Remember the **SABBATH** day, and keep it holy. (verse 8)
Honor your **FATHER** and your **MOTHER**. (verse 12)
You shall not **MURDER**. (verse 13)
You shall not **COMMIT** adultery. (verse 14)
You shall not **STEAL**. (verse 15)
You shall not bear **FALSE** witness against your neighbor. (verse 16)
You shall not **COVET**. (verse 17)

Reproducible 3C, "Our Awesome God"

When I look at your **HEAVENS**, the work of your **FINGERS**, the moon and the stars that you have established; what are human beings that you are mindful of them, mortals that you care for them? (Psalm 8:3-4)

The **HEAVENS** are telling the glory of God; and the firmament proclaims his **HANDIWORK**. (Psalm 19:1)

For the LORD, the Most High, is **AWESOME**, a great king over all the **EARTH**. (Psalm 47:2)

Reproducible 4B, "Life in Canaan"

Deborah used to sit under the palm of Deborah between **RAMAH** and **BETHEL** in the hill country of Ephraim; and the Israelites came up to her for judgment. (Judges 4:4–5)

Then Samuel said, "Gather all Israel at **MIZPAH**, and I will pray to the LORD for you." So they gathered at **MIZPAH**, . . . and said, "We have sinned against the LORD." And Samuel judged the people of Israel at **MIZPAH**.(1 Samuel 7:5–6)

David was king of Israel for forty years: he reigned seven years in **HEBRON**, and thirty-three years in **JERUSALEM**. (1 Kings 2:11)

•Reproducible 4C, "Micah's Message"

He has told you, O MORTAL, what is good; and what does the LORD REQUIRE of you but to do JUSTICE, and to love KINDNESS, and to WALK humbly with your God? (MICAH 6:8)

•Reproducible 4D, "Wise Words"

Solomon
This king wrote **3,000** proverbs and **1,005** songs.
A FRIEND loves at all times. (Proverbs 17:17a)
Train CHILDREN in the right way, and when old, they will not stray. (Proverbs 22:6)

•Reproducible 5A, "Jesus Is Born"

Read Luke 2:1-16: This gospel tells us that SHEPHERDS came to see Jesus, who was born in BETHLEHEM.
Read Matthew 2:1-11: This gospel tells that WISE MEN came to see Jesus, the king of the JEWS.

•Reproducible 5B, "Gospels"

Gospel means GOOD NEWS.
The Gospels tell us the good news about JESUS.
The four Gospel books in the Bible are: MATTHEW, MARK, LUKE, and JOHN.
The Gospels are in the NEW Testament.

•Reproducible 5C, "Miracle for a Multitude"

How many people offered a lunch to help Jesus feed the crowd? **1**
How many fish were in the lunch? **2**
How many baskets of food were left after everyone had eaten? **12**
How many people were in the crowd? **ABOUT 5,000**
How many loaves were in the lunch? **5**
How many people were fed that day? **ABOUT 5,000**

•Reproducible 5D, "Where Jesus Walked"

1. BETHLEHEM
2. NAZARETH
3. GALILEE
4. CAPERNAUM
5. JERICHO

•Reproducible 6B, "The Golden Rule"

DO TO OTHERS as you would have them **DO TO** you.

•Reproducible 6C, "Teachings of Jesus"

•Reproducible 7A, "The Church Is Born"

Soon after Jesus returned to God, his followers were all gathered in one place in Jerusalem to celebrate the spring harvest festival day of **PENTECOST** (Acts 2:1).

Suddenly the room where they were gathered was filled with a sound like the rush of a violent **WIND** (Acts 2:2). Then tongues of **FIRE** (Acts 2:3) appeared. All were filled with the **HOLY SPIRIT** (Acts 2:4) and began to speak in other languages.

Jews from many nations were living in Jerusalem. When they heard the followers of Jesus speaking, a crowd gathered. Everyone was bewildered, because each one heard them speaking in the native **LANGUAGE** of each (Acts 2:6).

Peter preached that day, telling everyone about Jesus. That day about **THREE THOUSAND** people were baptized and added as followers of Jesus. (Acts 2:41)

• Reproducible 7B, "Good Words from New Testament Letters"

For all who are **LED** by the Spirit of God are children of God. (Romans 8:14)

We know that all things work together for **GOOD** for those who love God. (Romans 8:28)

Do you not know that you are God's temple and that God's **SPIRIT** dwells in you? (1 Corinthians 3:16)

I **THANK** my God every time I remember you. (Philippians 1:3)

Beloved, let us **LOVE** one another; because love is from God. (1 John 4:7)

• Reproducible 7C, "Some Early Christian Leaders"

PETER said to them, "Repent, and be baptized every one of you in the name of Jesus Christ..." (Acts 2:38)

One day Peter and **JOHN** were going up to the temple at the hour of prayer. (Acts 3:1)

STEPHEN, full of grace and power, did great wonders and signs among the people. (Acts 6:8)

PHILIP went down to the city of Samaria and proclaimed the Messiah to them. (Acts 8:5)

Now in Joppa there was a disciple whose name was Tabitha, which in Greek is **DORCAS**. She was devoted to good works and acts of charity. (Acts 9:36)

As soon as he realized this, he went to the house of **MARY**, the mother of John...where many had gathered and were praying. (Acts 12:12)

After some days **PAUL** said to **BARNABAS**, "Come let us return and visit the believers in every city where we proclaimed the word of the Lord and see how they are doing." (Acts 15:36)

Reproducible 7D, "The Good News Spreads"

Reproducible 8A, "Great Inventions"

PICTURE WRITING	SCROLLS	BIBLE
ALPHABETS	CODEX BOOKS	
PAPYRUS	PRINTING PRESS	
PARCHMENT	PAPER	

Reproducible 8C, "How Our Bible Began"

ORAL TRADITION	LETTERS
OLD TESTAMENT	GOSPEL
NEW TESTAMENT	WRITTEN

Reproducible 8D, "One Book, Many Languages"

HEBREW	GREEK	ENGLISH
GREEK	LATIN	GERMAN
HEBREW	GREEK	INDIA
GREEK	HEBREW	LANGUAGES